KAIJUMAX
SEASON ONE

KAIJ

KAIJUMAX
TERROR and RESPECT
• SEASON ONE •
怪獣マックス
By Zander Cannon
Color flatting by Jason Fischer
Designed by Fred Chao
Logo by Zander Cannon
Edited by Charlie Chu
ONI PRESS
An Oni Press Publication

Published by Oni Press, Inc.
Joe Nozemack, publisher
James Lucas Jones, editor in chief
Cheyenne Allott, director of sales
Amber O'Neill, marketing coordinator
Rachel Reed, publicity coordinator
Troy Look, director of design & production
Hilary Thompson, graphic designer
Jared Jones, digital art technician
Charlie Chu, senior editor
Robin Herrera, editor
Ari Yarwood, editor
Bess Pallares, editorial assistant
Brad Rooks, director of logistics
Jung Lee, office assistant

onipress.com
facebook.com/onipress
twitter.com/onipress
onipress.tumblr.com
instagram.com/onipress

zandercannon.com / @zander_cannon

KAIJUMAX.COM

studiojfish.com / @studiojfish

This volume collects issues #1-6 of the Oni Press series Kaijumax.

First edition: February 2016

ISBN 978-1-62010-270-1
eISBN 978-1-62010-271-8

PRINTED IN CHINA.

Library of Congress Control Number: 2015948983

3 4 5 6 7 8 9 10

episode 1

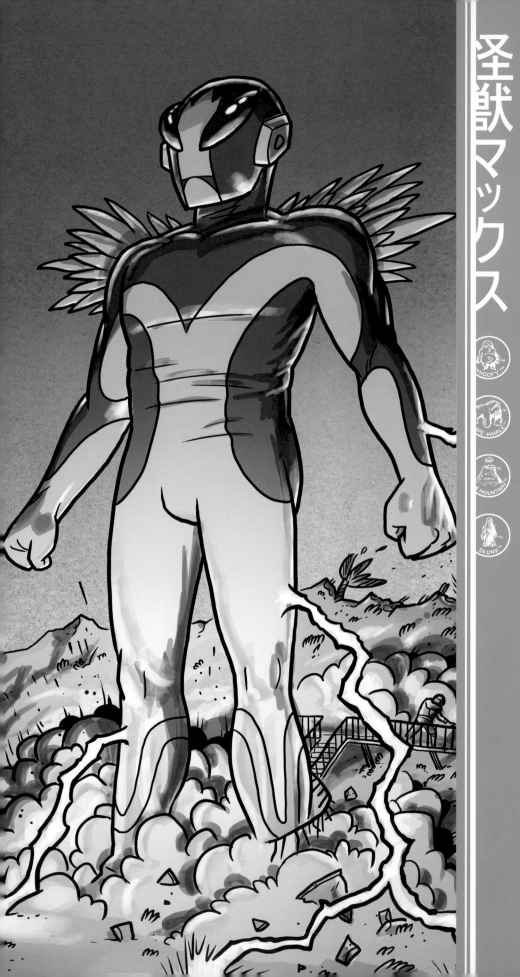

圣獣マックス

MONDAY 0700
Y-you think this... iron rope... give you the RIGHT, little man?
You think... you all so... so power-have. So smash. You... you think you KING!

Shut it, cloaker.
That chain doesn't give me jack. It's THIS that gives me the power here. So respect it.
And learn the language.

Attention inmates.
You will make land here, then follow the line up the hill to INTAKE.
ENTRANCE
Y-YOU ALL THINK YOU'RE SO BIG.
YOU ALL THINK YOU'RE SO RIGHT.

Any failure to obey will be interpreted as aggression and dealt with accordingly.
I WAS ONLY TRYING TO FEED MY CHILDREN.
I NEED TO GET BACK TO THEM. THEY'RE HUNGRY AND SCARED.

SNIFF
YOU'RE THE ONES WHO SHOULD BE PUNISHED.
INTAKE
INTAKE
YOU'RE THE ONES WHO SHOULD BE TAKEN AWAY FROM YOUR FAMILIES.
Y-YOU ALL...

YOU'RE THE MONSTERS!!

怪獣MAX TERROR & RESPECT

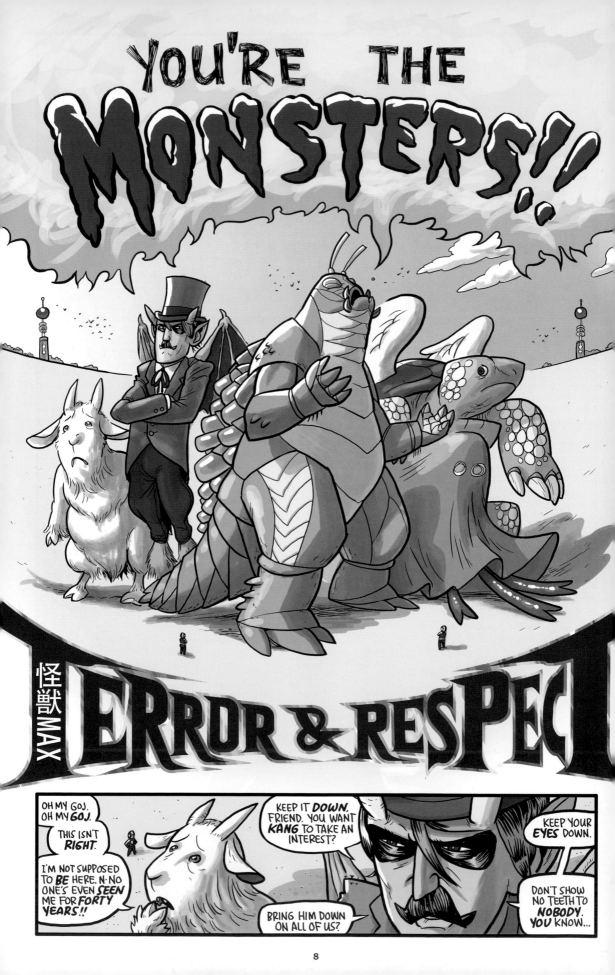

THERE'S A **J-POP** FOR APE-WHALE'S CREW, A **SPACE CASE**, A CRYP WHO'S SCARED OF HIS OWN **SHADOW**, AND UH...

YEAH.

LAST GUY'S **INTERESTING**. **"ELECTROGOR"**. NEVER SEEN HIM BEFORE, BUT WORD IS HE'S **HARD**.

"...THEY SAY HE'S A **FAMILY MAN**."
I DON'T THINK HE'S COMING **BACK**.

SURE HE IS. OF **COURSE** HE IS. C'MON, IT'S **DAD**. HE WOULDN'T LEAVE US **OVERNIGHT**.

HE'S GOING TO BE BACK IN JUST A FEW MINUTES JUICED WITH ALL THE FOOD WE COULD **WANT**.

AND A GREAT STORY ABOUT WHAT **TOOK** SO LONG.

YEAH, BUT **TORGAX**, HE WAS SUPPOSED TO--
VOGO!!
LOOK OU--

VOGO!! VOGO, NO!!
OH GOJ, TORGAX, HE'S--
" Snap OUT of it. "

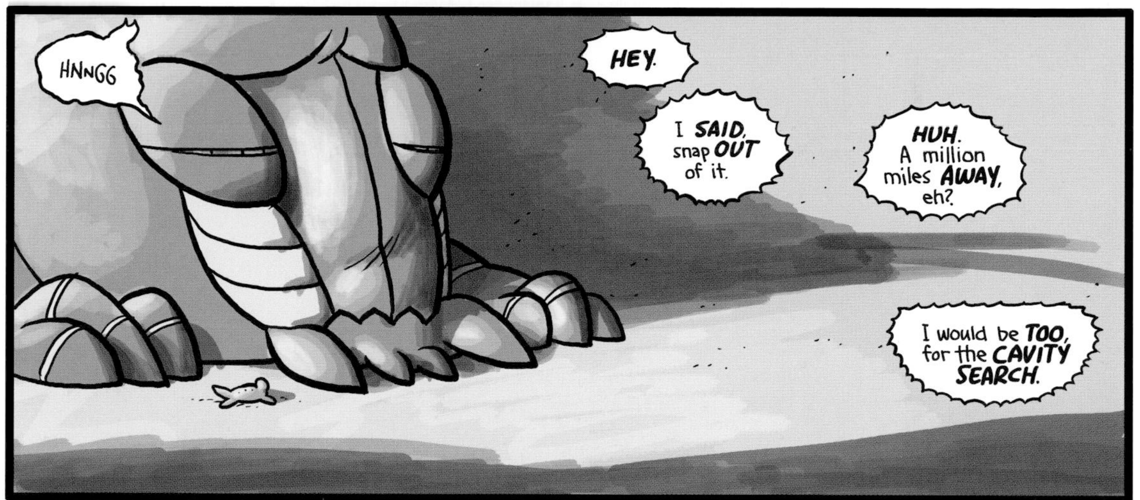
HNNGG
HEY.
I SAID, snap OUT of it.
HUH. A million miles AWAY, eh?
I would be TOO, for the CAVITY SEARCH.

You caused a big FUSS when you arrived, going ON and ON.
"Children" this, "children" THAT.
All of your FRIENDS have moved ON to their CRATERS in GEN-POP, but now YOU...

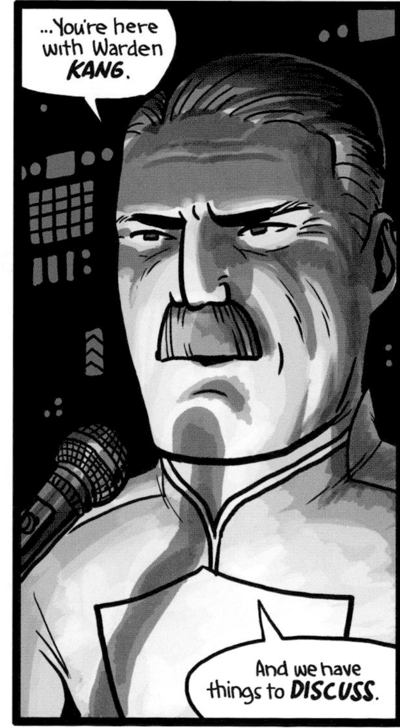
...You're here with Warden KANG.
And we have things to DISCUSS.

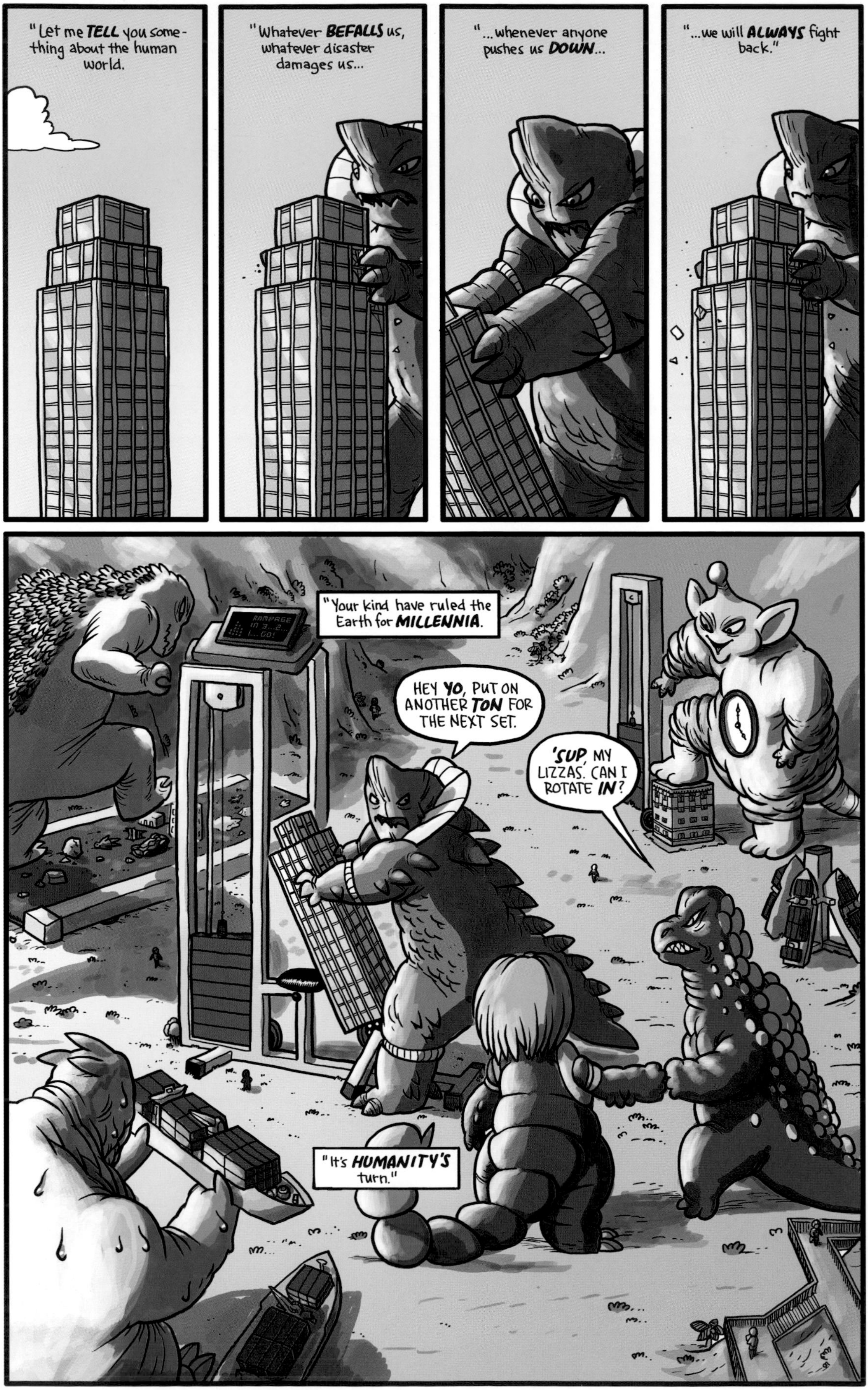

"Your kind have ruled the Earth for **MILLENNIA**.

HEY **YO**, PUT ON ANOTHER **TON** FOR THE NEXT SET.

'SUP, MY LIZZAS. CAN I ROTATE **IN**?

"It's **HUMANITY'S** turn."

And we will bring down the HAMMER to defend our POSITION.
The hammer in this case being our friend JEONG.
He's not inclined to be GENTLE when you're found chewing on a Trans-Pacific CABLE, I'm afraid.
JEONG

"It's a difficult world out there. COMPLICATED. And no longer FIT for you."
ZÜÜÜÜ! REEL 'EM IN! NEW BRODO ASOGIANS, COMING THROUGH!
WHAT'RE YOU GOING TO DO, CALL HOME?

"Our RULES keep everyone in line."

"Keep the weak safe from the STRONG."

This is the ONLY place for you and your kind.
The LAST place on Earth.
Now LOOK up here and TELL me:

Where...
...are your CHILDREN?

UH, **HEY**. WE CAME IN TOGETHER.
I GUESS WE'RE **CRATER-MATES**.
I'M **ELECTROGOR**.

YEAH. **HI**. I'M THE **CREATURE** FROM **DEVIL'S CREEK**.
NICE TO--

UH, YOU ALL RIGHT?
YOUR FACE LOOKS KIND OF... **SINGED**, OR SOMETHING.

UH, UH... L-**LISTEN**.
I-I HEARD YOU TALKIN' ABOUT YOUR **KIDS**. HOW YOU NEED TO GET TO 'EM. OR, UH, UH, **TALK** TO 'EM.
S-SO I GOTTA **TELL** YOU SOMETHING. UH...
W-WELL, THERE'S A **GUY**. M-MIGHT COULD HELP YOU.

H-HE'S IN THE NORTH GLADE. THAT'S KAI-BLOCK.
I, UH, I THINK HE'S LEAVING SOON. YOU MIGHT WANT TO TRY TO CATCH HIM.

HUH. YEAH. YEAH. THANKS. I WILL.
I GUESS YOU'RE LEARNING FAST ABOUT THIS PLACE.

UH...
SERIOUSLY, ARE YOU ALL RIGHT?

I UH...I GUESS IT'S CALLED A FIRE CHECK.
GET YOU WITH FIRE, SEE IF YOU FIGHT BACK.

DID YOU FIGHT BACK?

...
...NO...

W-WELL, HEY LISTEN, MAYBE THAT'S BEST, Y'KNOW?
THESE LIFE-CYCLERS-- WHO KNOWS WHAT THEY'LL DO IF YOU STOMP TO THEM?
YEAH...

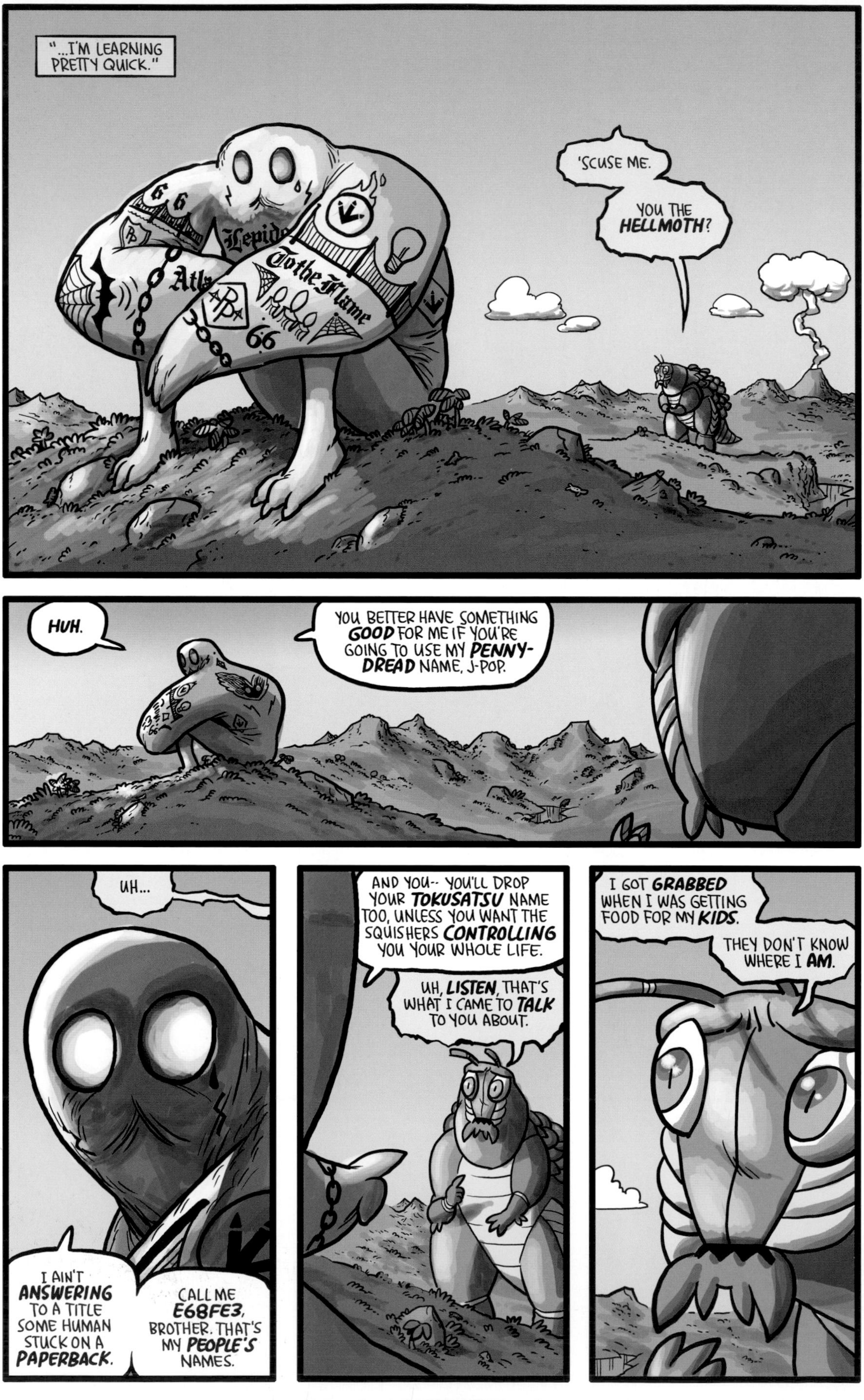

"...I'M LEARNING PRETTY QUICK."
'SCUSE ME.
YOU THE **HELLMOTH**?

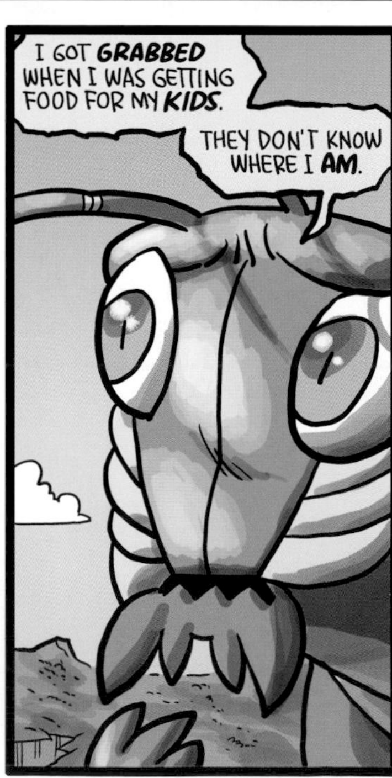

I NEED SOMEONE TO CHECK ON THEM.
THEY'RE IN A CAVE ON AN ISLAND IN THE BERING SEA. TH-THE ALEUTIAN ISLANDS-- THAT'S WHAT THE HUMANS CALL THEM.

THEY'RE GOING TO BE SCARED.
I'M GOING TO TRY TO GET OUT OF HERE AS SOON AS I CAN, BUT I NEED THEM TO KNOW WHAT'S GOING ON.

WHY SHOULD I DO IT?
THIS PLACE HAS GOT NOTHING ON ME NOW. I DON'T NEED THE HEAT.

PLEASE. THE BIG MAN-- KANG-- KNOWS THEY'RE OUT THERE.
THEY KNOW IT'S CLOSE TO WHERE THEY GOT ME.

HE WANTS TO BRING THEM HERE.
WHAT IF HE BRINGS MY KIDS HERE, TO THIS HORRIBLE PLACE, WITH ALL THESE--

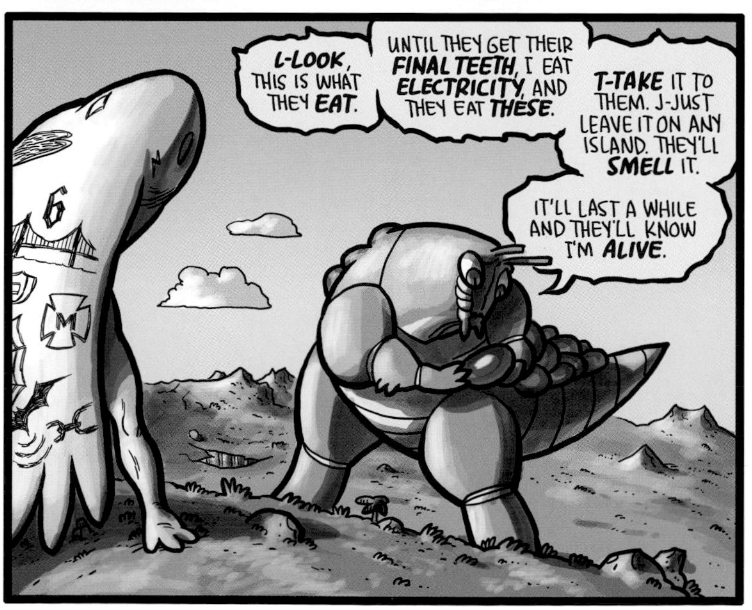
L-LOOK, THIS IS WHAT THEY EAT.
UNTIL THEY GET THEIR FINAL TEETH, I EAT ELECTRICITY, AND THEY EAT THESE.
T-TAKE IT TO THEM. J-JUST LEAVE IT ON ANY ISLAND. THEY'LL SMELL IT.
IT'LL LAST A WHILE AND THEY'LL KNOW I'M ALIVE.

Y-YOU CAN HAVE SOME TOO.
IT'S U-235. I DON'T KNOW IF YOU LIKE THAT, OR--
HOLD ON, HOLD ON.

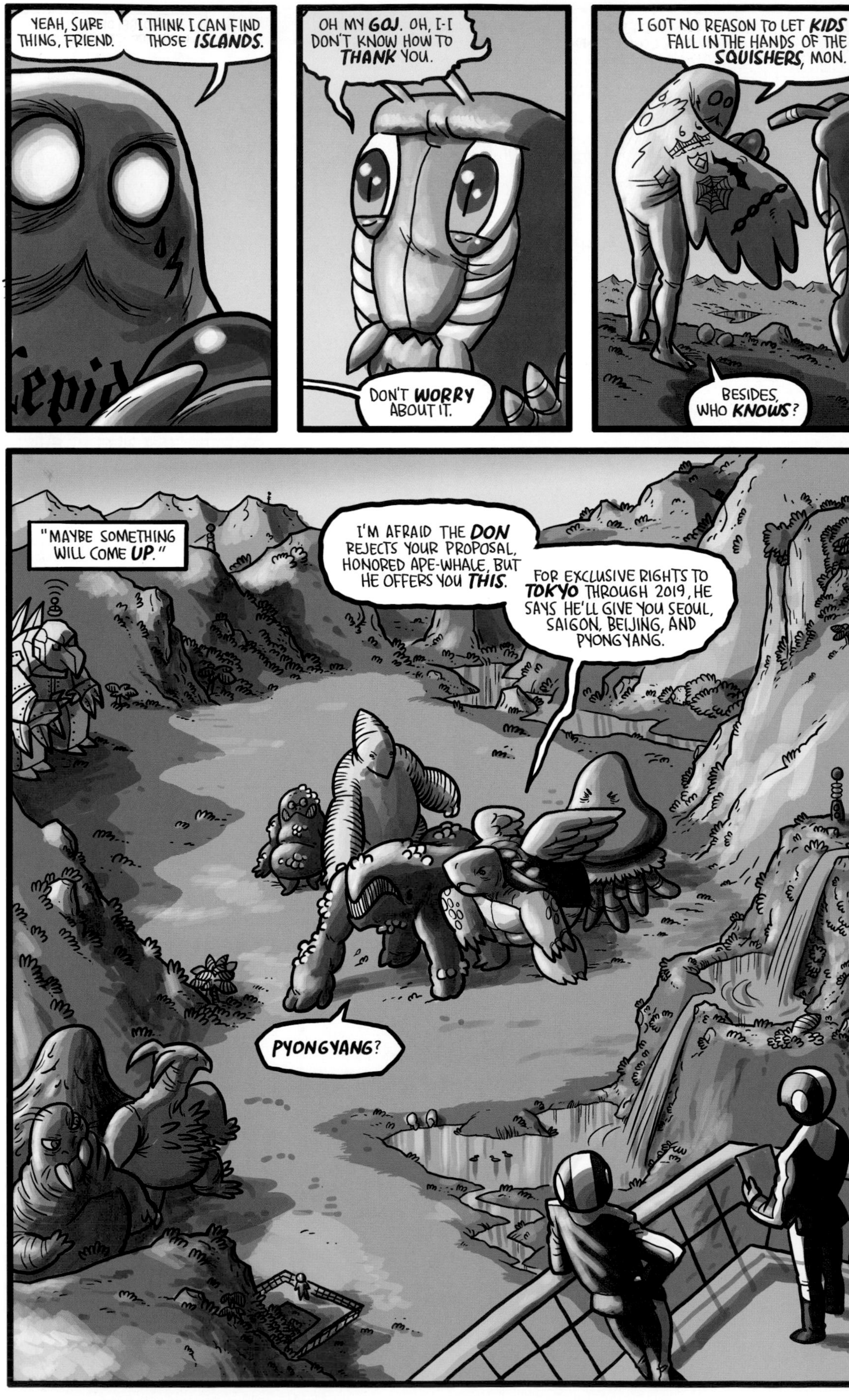

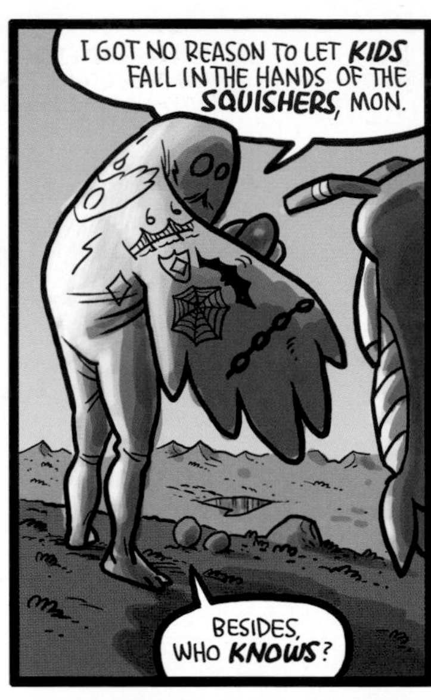

"MAYBE SOMETHING WILL COME **UP**."

I'M AFRAID THE **DON** REJECTS YOUR PROPOSAL, HONORED APE-WHALE, BUT HE OFFERS YOU **THIS**.

FOR EXCLUSIVE RIGHTS TO **TOKYO** THROUGH 2019, HE SAYS HE'LL GIVE YOU SEOUL, SAIGON, BEIJING, AND PYONGYANG.

PYONGYANG?

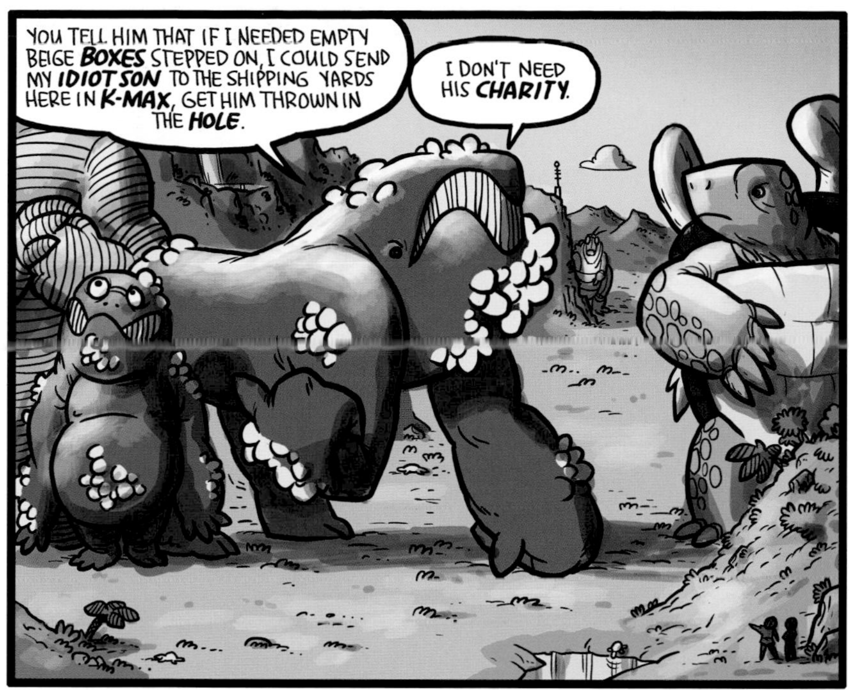
YOU TELL HIM THAT IF I NEEDED EMPTY BEIGE BOXES STEPPED ON, I COULD SEND MY IDIOT SON TO THE SHIPPING YARDS HERE IN K-MAX, GET HIM THROWN IN THE HOLE.
I DON'T NEED HIS CHARITY.

TOKYO BELONGS TO US. WE'LL BE STOMPING FOR HIM THE SECOND WE WALK OUT OF THIS PLACE.
HEY THERE. GETTING THE LAY OF THE LAND?

HM?
THAT HAS-BEEN.
HIS ZOOKY-ASS KID.

ALL IT WOULD TAKE IS A SECOND WHERE EVERYONE LOOKS THE OTHER WAY, A SHARPENED HULL IN YOUR HAND...

...AND PHHT.

WHO ARE YOU?
I'M THE ONE WHO'S GOT YOUR FULL ATTENTION.

SO.
LOOKS LIKE WE DID YOU A **FAVOR** BACK THERE.

MY BUDDY DON'T **LIKE** THAT NAME. BUT **YEAH**. AND NOW YOU **OWE** US, MEGAFAUNA.
HERE'S HOW IT PLAYS **OUT**.

"THOSE **J-POP** CLOAKERS HAVE RUN THIS PLACE SINCE YOU WAS JUST A **TWINKLE** AT THE BOTTOM OF THE **SEA**."

"THAT'S NOT **HAPPENING** NO MORE. **THIS** IS. THE CRYPS ARE MOVING **UP**."

"THEY THINK WE DON'T GOT THE **NUMBERS**, BUT YOU DON'T **NEED** BIG NUMBERS WHEN THE ONES YOU GOT ARE IN THE RIGHT **PLACES**."

SOMETHING **LOUD'S** GONNA GO DOWN OVER THERE.
YOU GOT **THREE MINUTES**. THE OLD MAN AND THE **HALF-WIT**. BOSS WANTS 'EM INSIDE **OUT**.

A LIZZER DOES IT **RIGHT**, THINGS COULD LOOK **ROSY** FOR YOU WITH THE CRYPS.
WE GOT **ONE** GUY OUT ON A TECHNICALITY. MAYBE WE COULD DO IT **AGAIN**.
FIJI ★ PETROLEUM

BUT DO IT **WRONG**, YOU'LL FIND OUT HOW **MANY** EYES-- AND **SHANKS**-- WE GOT IN THIS HOLE.

NOT TO **MENTION** OUT IN THE **WORLD**.

YOUR HEART IS **HEAVY**, BROTHER.
WH--?

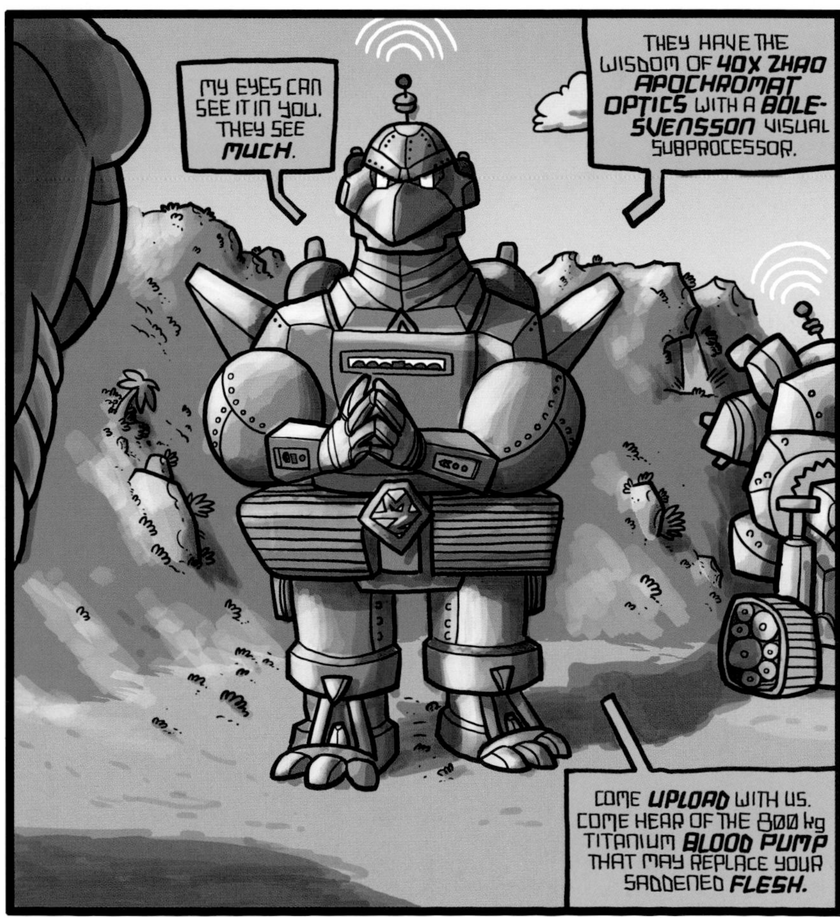
MY EYES CAN SEE IT IN YOU. THEY SEE **MUCH**.
THEY HAVE THE WISDOM OF **40X ZHAO APOCHROMAT OPTICS** WITH A **BOLE-SVENSSON** VISUAL SUBPROCESSOR.
COME **UPLOAD** WITH US. COME HEAR OF THE 800 kg TITANIUM **BLOOD PUMP** THAT MAY REPLACE YOUR SADDENED **FLESH**.

ANOTHER TIME, PERHAPS.

IN THE PRESENCE OF THE CLOUD, BROTHER, YOU NEEDN'T WORRY ABOUT WHO IS STRONGEST. ABOUT WHO IS BIGGEST.
ABOUT WHO IS KING.

I SAID ANOTHER TIME.
HEY MECHA-ZONN!

WHY DON'T YOU CUT OUT THAT TIN-LIZZA CRAP YOU'RE CLANKIN' AWAY ABOUT?
WE HEARD IT ALL BEFORE ABOUT YOUR STUPID THING IN THE SKY!
YEAH! SOUNDS LIKE 'GOTO 10, GOTO 10, GOTO 10'!!

WHY DON'T YOU GO BACK TO THE LAB, YOU LOAD-LIFTERS?
YOU'RE SMELLIN' THE PLACE UP LIKE ETHANOL!

WHY YOU FORTEAN MEGAF--
NO! NO, MY BROTHERS. THEIR FLESH IS WEAK. THEY KNOW NO BETTER.
WE DO. WE--
ZT ZAT

NO--
KSSHZZZZT!!

STOMP THOSE REDKING CLOUD-THUMPERS!

WHAT is going ON?!!
WARDEN! They just--
NEVER MIND! I'LL handle this...!

ALL of you--
STOP THIS IMMEDIATELY!
I SAID: ALL OF YOU--

STOP THIS
IMMED Y

OH MY **GOJ**--

GO! GO! **MOVE!**

CHK

ALL OF YOU. YOU ARE PARTICIPATING IN AN UNLAWFUL RIOT.
RETURN TO YOUR CRATERS NOW OR YOU'LL BUY YOURSELF A DAY IN THE--
WAIT.
STOP, BROTHER. WHAT ARE YOU DOING?
SHUT UP AND SIT DOWN, YOU REDKING 'NILLA!

YOU. THE ONE THAT WOULDN'T TALK.
YOU'VE GOT NOTHING TO DO WITH THIS.
GET BACK IN LINE.

DON'T.
DON'T EVEN LOOK AT ME, YOU TRENCH-DWELLING SACK OF INK.
I SAID, BACK IN LINE.

I'M WARNING YOU.
I'M WARNING YOU.
GET BACK IN--

...LINE...

HOOOOURGH
WHAT IN THE FLOATING CONTINENT--?

WHAT ARE YOU DOING

DVVVVVV

HNNGH!!
VZEEE

CHAKK
WHAT'S HE--
OH GOJ--

WOOSH WOOSH
OH--
THAT POOR SPAWN OF A--
OH I'M GONNA BE SICK
BLEEUB
FOOOSH

SHONNG

NOW--
ALL OF YOU.

BACK TO YOUR CRATERS

Get on the wrong end of KANG and it'll BITE you, huh?

HNNGG
A week in SOLITARY.
THAT'S a nice way to start.
Well, don't worry about it too much.

It's all about DECISIONS in here. I've made a few doozies in MY time too.

I'm GUPTA, by the way.

H'M EGGR.
Ah, I'll get it from you LATER.
We'll both be around a while, won't we?

The HOLE.
Anyway, here we ARE.
Lotta time to THINK in there, y'know.
So think about THIS.

We get all KINDS here at KAIJUMAX.
For EXAMPLE, there was this TOWN in AMERICA. Kleinberg HEIGHTS.

It's not THERE anymore. Just wiped off the MAP.
Oh, we GOT the mon who did it.

BIG.
WHITE.
LOTTA INK ON HIS WINGS.
But we had to let him GO.
TODAY, in fact.
A TECHNICALITY.

No WITNESSES.
Word is he sniffed 'em out and ATE 'em all.

MEN, WOMEN, CHILDREN, LIVE-STOCK, PETS, you NAME it.
Probably CARS too, for all I know.
Now who KNOWS where he could be heading, ELECTROGOR.

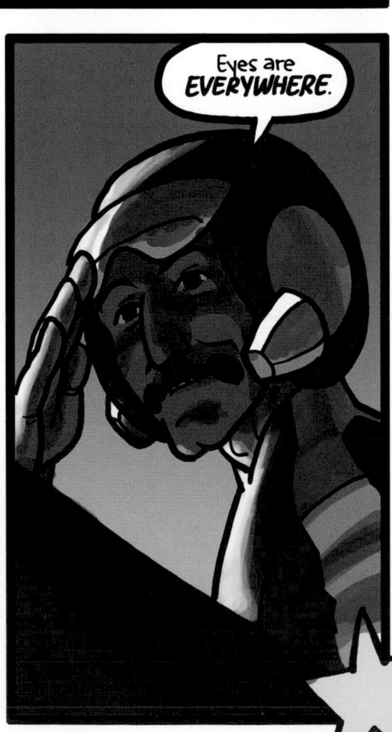
Eyes are EVERYWHERE.

episode

2

怪獣マックス

PRISONER INTAKE
TUESDAY, 8 AM.
GUPTA here.
Okay, I'm banking right at the ILEAL CLIFFS.
Looks like we've got a reading here, pretty WEAK.

Nothing yet, but he's one of APE-WHALE'S boys, so I'm willing to BET--
--Hold on.

ECCH.
Yeah, here we GO.
I guess the word got OUT about the attempt on the big man's LIFE.
Sure ENOUGH, he's Cristoed something UP in here.
Looks like a RADIO TOWER, wrapped in... a SAIL, and maybe a SQUID?

OKAY, I got it HITCHED. Bracing the ship for the big YANK.
HA. Yeah, you got THAT right, brother. I hope it DOES hurt him.

NNF
OKAY. Almost AROUND.
Bringing it out NOW.

UHHGGH. This part is the WORST.
Almost OUT...

CAREFUL...

BLECH.

HEY!!

Got a **WEAPON** here!!

All right, cloaker, get it **MOVING.** You'll be pulling down extra **TIME** for tryin' this crap with us.

TEN THOUSAND YEARS to LIFE

YOU GUYS ARE DOING GREAT.
TORGAX! YOU'RE SWIMMING PERFECTLY NOW!
" "!!
THE LEG'S HEALED UP! YOU'D NEVER KNOW YOU WERE EVER HURT, HONEY!
GIVE YOU A LITTLE TIME, AND YOU'LL BE SWIMMING FASTER THAN--

...G.R.E.A.T. Action Ship reporting, on a magnetic heading of 120...
...investigating a WHALING VESSEL'S incident report from last month. Nothing CONCLUSIVE but...
--THAN--

KIDS. GET BACK TO THE CAVE. DO NOT SURFACE.
...originating above ocean FLOOR, at 52 Hz, we're getting a COUPLE blips here...
AW, DAD! IT'S GROSS DOWN THERE AND--
USE THE UNDER-ENTRANCE.
DAD, WHAT ARE YOU DOING? DON'T GO UP THERE!

THEY'VE GOT OUR LOCATION, HONEY.
AND NO ONE HURTS MY LITTLE GIRL.
I'LL BE RIGHT BACK.

...whalers are saying they took a CHUNK out of it. They -- hold on.
Yeah. Got a SPIKE.
G.R.E.A.T.
In a minute we can get you a full IMAGING.

...data's COMPILING-- looks like we've got a--
HOLY MOTHER OF GOD
"Time's UP."

So, your CHILDREN– what are they?
I mean, uh, are they BOYS, or...
ONE is boy. He SMALL. Other NOT-SMALL. She is GIRL.

YOU. You is GOOD.
What?
I's BRAIN say to me: you is a good SQUISHER-- uh, HUMAN.
You is KIND.
I's CHILDS. I is scared they is HURT.

YOU?
You're SCARED...?
sniff

PLEASE. They in DANGER.
You-- YOU go back? Go to I's ISLAND. CALL them. Say I's NAME.
Bring them FOOD.
Whoa, whoa. HOLD on.

I'm not going ANYWHERE. I'm a GUARD, not a FIELD AGENT.
Talk to JEONG. Or GUPTA maybe. See if THEY--
NO!!

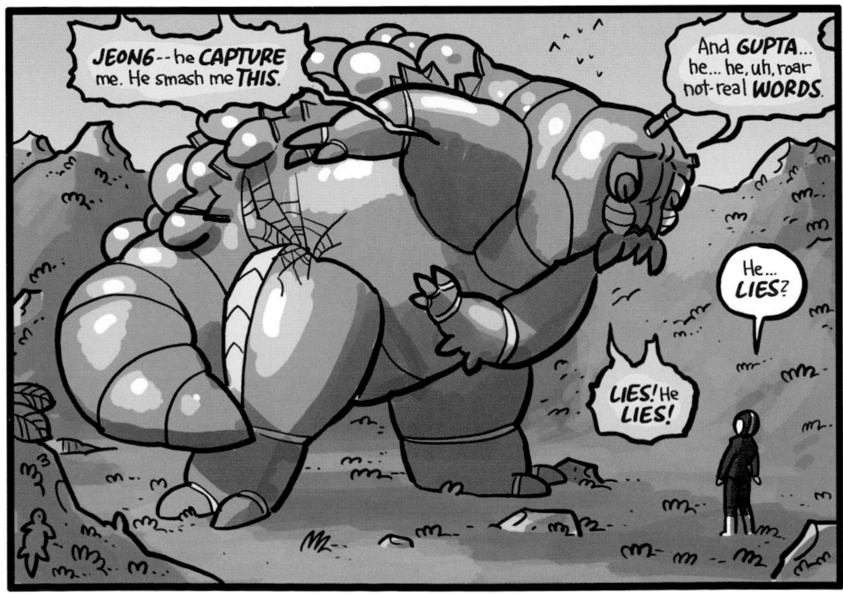

JEONG-- he CAPTURE me. He smash me THIS.
And GUPTA... he... he, uh, roar not-real WORDS.
He... LIES?
LIES! He LIES!

But you... you NOT-BAD human. You clean pods in SOLITARY. You LOOK, you see if they OKAY!

Look, I mean, I can pass it up the CHAIN to Warden KANG, at the MEETING today, and maybe he'll send some --
N-NO! Not KANG.
KANG want to put them in CAGE. He put them in HERE. With all of these... what you say? CLOAKERS?

Hhhh
LISTEN, inmate.
I'm a little TIRED of hearing about all the BRIDGES you've burned.
You seem DECENT and all-- more of an ANTI-HERO or a force of NATURE than a BAD GUY...

... but what KANG wants, that's ME, too. I'm not going to go outside my JOB, outside the LAW.
Your kids are lost in a big, ugly WORLD that doesn't WANT them. Maybe what they NEED is to come here.

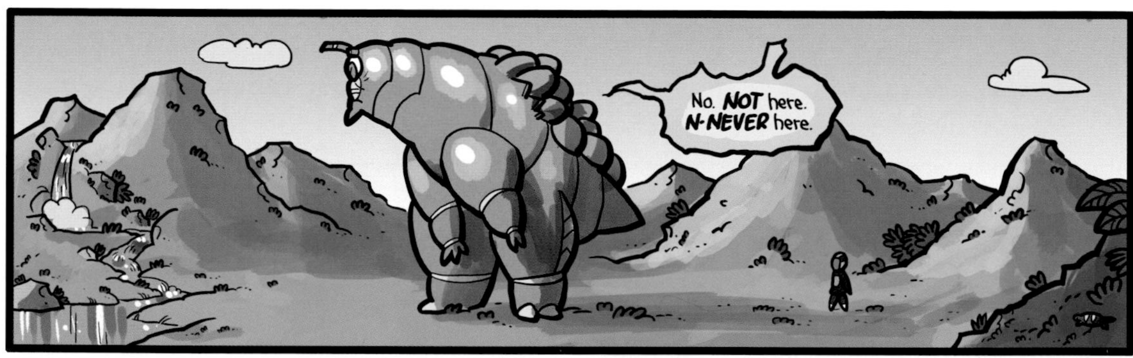
No. NOT here. N-NEVER here.

"Here TERRIBLE."
CHECK-IN
GUPTA

SHING

VOOM

HUSH!
宇都宮 SHIPPING

HEY!
I SAID SHUT **UP!**

'SUP, MON?
GUPTA! Y-YO, MAN, WHERE YOU **BEEN?**
L-LIKE, I'M N-NEEDIN' THAT **STUFF**, KYODAI. GOT A **SEISMIC EVENT** GOIN' ON HERE, KNOW WHAT I'M **SAYIN'?**

WELL, I GOT IT IF YOU GOT THE **MONEY**, 'NILLA.
D-DON'T BE **CALLING** ME THAT, KYO. THAT AIN'T **ME**, THAT AIN'T WHAT I'M **LIKE**. I JUST NEED A LITTLE **CRACKLE** TO GET ME THROUGH, THAT'S ALL.
B-BUT I MEAN **YEAH**, I GOT THE MONEY.

ALL RIGHT THEN...
YEAH, H-HERE YOU GO. FIFTY YAP-RAI.
AND THERE YOU ARE.

HNFFF
SO. THE REST OF YOU.
UH...
WELL, WHAT YOU GOT, SQUISHER?
ANYTHING GOOD, OR JUST THE DITCH-VOLTS YOU ALWAYS TRYIN' TO PUSH OFF ON US?

YOU CAN CRAM IT RIGHT UP YOUR ULTRA-ZONE, LIZZER.
TAKE YOUR BUSINESS TO THE COMPETITION IF YOU DON'T LIKE IT.
I GOT ELECTRICITY-- INDUSTRIAL GENERATORS THIS TIME-- SMOG, MAGIC STONES, DIOXIN--
I-I'LL TAKE SOME SMOG.

NEW GUY, HUH? THAT'S WHAT I'M TALKIN' ABOUT.
YEAH, TAKE THE EDGE OFF, GOATSE.
SCREW THAT. WHAT ABOUT THE U, FOOL?

LISTEN. URANIUM'S HARD TO COME BY THESE DAYS. THE SUPPLY CHAIN'S HAD A HICCUP.
YOU LISTEN. I DON'T EVEN KNOW WHAT A HICCUP IS. YOU GOT AN ISLAND FULL OF LIZZAS AND THEY OVER-FIENDIN' FOR THAT U, YOU FEEL ME?
YOU GOT A JOB TO LOSE IF SOMEONE WEREN'T CAREFUL WHAT AND WHEN THEY BE ROARIN', LIKE.

THAP

SHRIP

NNUH
WHAT--

BLAT

YOU GET THIS AND YOU GET THIS GOOD. NOBODY THREATENS ME. YOU THINK YOUR LIFE-CYCLE'S BAD NOW?
I'LL MAKE THE NEXT TEN THOUSAND YEARS A REDKING NIGHTMARE, 'NILLA. YOU'LL BEG ME TO PUT AN OXYGEN DESTROYER IN YOUR MOUTH.

HKKTHT!!
HEY! HEY! COOL IT! GOT ANOTHER HACK COMING!

THUD

IT'S JUST...
...JUST GONNA GROW BACK, CLOAKER...
DON'T I KNOW IT.

I ONLY WISH THERE WAS A WAY TO GET RID OF YOU ALL FOR GOOD.

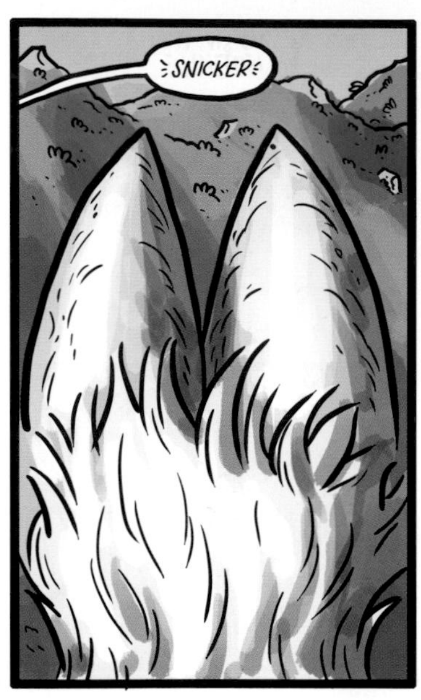
SNICKER

KOFF
OH MAN, IT'S LIKE WHOOOAAH NESSIE...
HEY.

WHOA.
HEY MON, MY CRATERMATE. ELECTROGOR. WHAT'S UP. YOU'RE BACK. COOL.
WHAT'S UUUUUUP.

!!
THAP

HNNF!
WHAM

DO YOU KNOW WHAT YOU DID?
DO YOU KNOW WHAT YOU DID TO ME??
THE CRYPTIDS ARE THE WORST GANG IN THIS AMBERGRIS-HOLE.
YOUR "TIP" PUT ME IN THEIR DEBT. ON THEIR BAD SIDE.

KRAK

I'LL REDKING TEAR YOU APART. DO YOU UNDERSTAND WHAT IT MEANS TO BE UNDERWATER WITH THEM?
DO YOU?

AND IF THERE'S ONE THING I'VE LEARNED ABOUT THE CRYPS...

"...YOU DON'T DENY THEM."
OH MARIANAS NO. YOU AIN'T WELCOME HERE, HACK.
WHOA, WHOA! DON'T BE TALKING SO HASTY, MY MINOR CLONE!

THIS ONE IS OUR BUDDY. HE TAKES CARE OF US!
GUPTA, WHAT ARE YOU UP TO, MY BIG GREEN LIZZA?!
LISTEN, ZLOOK...

...I AIN'T NO LIZZA.
YOUR MAMA MAY RUN THE CRYSTAL EMPIRE ON THE OUTSIDE...
...BUT YOU STILL TALK TO ME RESPECTFULLY IN HERE OR WE'RE GONNA HAVE A REAL PROBLEM.
OH, NOW, NO NEED FOR THAT, KYODAI.
WE DON'T GOT TO BE BATTLING, USING OUR SPECIAL MOVES ON EACH OTHER, DO WE?

YOU ARE ALWAYS WELCOME HERE. COME AND GO AS YOU ARE PLEASING.
NOW, I KNOW YOU ARE BRINGING ME THINGS. GOOD THINGS.
THINGS FIT FOR A PRINCE.

ALL RIGHT THEN.
I GOT SOME PACKS OF SMOKESTACKS FOR YOU ALL IN HERE.
SOME CERNE ABBAS HILLSIDES..? I DUNNO, SOME OF YOUR BOYS MIGHT BE INTO THAT...
WHAT ELSE, MAN?

I GRABBED A FEW MORE MEGALODONS FROM THE CHOW LINE. YOU HUNGRY?
HA HA!
NAH, SERIOUSLY, MAN, MY FRIEND, MY SPACE BROTHER...
...WHAT DO YOU HAVE FOR ME?

OKAY, LISTEN.
I KNOW WHAT YOU'RE ASKING FOR. YOUR MOTHER IS PRETTY SPECIFIC ABOUT IT. SHE DOES NOT WANT YOU GETTING MIXED UP WITH DRUGS.
HA HA! NOW YOU LISTEN.

EVERYONE KNOWS I'M A VON VILESTRA, SO THEY RESPECT ME, AND THEY LEAVE ME BE. NO VENTRAL INDIGNITIES.
BUT STILL THE DAYS GO BY VERY SLOW, YOU KNOW, MAN? THAT IS THE SORT OF THING THAT IS NOT EASY.
DO YOU WANT ME TO BE TELLING HER THAT YOU ARE NOT DOING YOUR JOB MAKING THIS PLACE EASY FOR ME, SPACE BRO?

HHH
THIS IS ALL I CAN GIVE YOU.
SHUSH!
I SAID BE QUIET.

OH, COME ON.
ARE YOU KIDDING ME?

VIRGINS?
THAT'S LIKE OLD TIMES, BRO!
WHO EVEN DOES THAT STUFF ANY-MORE?
SHUT UP, KID. THEY'LL GET YA HIGH.
PSSH. BARELY. ALL RIGHT, WHAT-EVER, MAN.

OH GOD!
NO! PLEASE!
HELP!

MNCH MNCH GULP
SO. THANKS, BUT I NEED SOMETHING MORE NEXT TIME.
KNOW WHAT I MEAN, MAN? YOU ARE GOOD, BUT DON'T LET ME DOWN OR MOTHER WILL KNOW.
SO. RUN ALONG NOW.

MY LITTLE KYODAI SERVANT.

Now that GUPTA'S finally here, we can START.
So listen UP. We got a lot to COVER here, and not much TIME.
Item ONE:
Next WEEK, this facility will be getting an INSPECTION from MATSUMOTO.

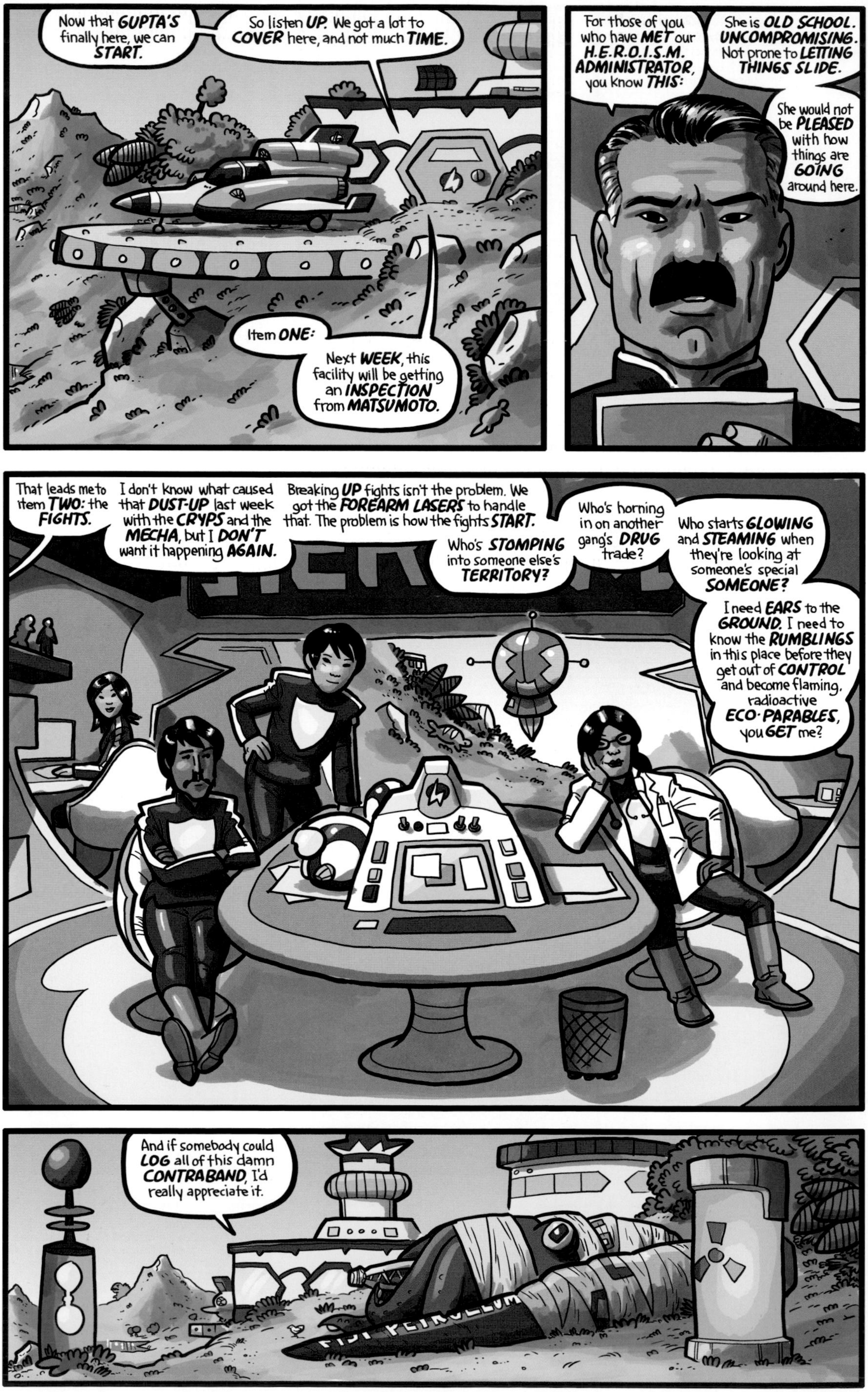

For those of you who have MET our H.E.R.O.I.S.M. ADMINISTRATOR, you know THIS:
She is OLD SCHOOL. UNCOMPROMISING. Not prone to LETTING THINGS SLIDE.
She would not be PLEASED with how things are GOING around here.

That leads me to item TWO: the FIGHTS.
I don't know what caused that DUST-UP last week with the CRYPS and the MECHA, but I DON'T want it happening AGAIN.
Breaking UP fights isn't the problem. We got the FOREARM LASERS to handle that. The problem is how the fights START.
Who's STOMPING into someone else's TERRITORY?
Who's horning in on another gang's DRUG trade?
Who starts GLOWING and STEAMING when they're looking at someone's special SOMEONE?
I need EARS to the GROUND. I need to know the RUMBLINGS in this place before they get out of CONTROL and become flaming, radioactive ECO-PARABLES, you GET me?

And if somebody could LOG all of this damn CONTRABAND, I'd really appreciate it.

Right, item THREE.
TELSTAR ROBOT KEIKO-CHAN tells me that we are experiencing an unusual amount of RADIOACTIVITY throughout the PRISON.
KEIKO? You want to EXPAND on that?

YES, SIR. MY SENSORS ARE UNABLE TO TRIANGULATE THE SOURCE OF THE ACTIVITY, BUT OUR SECURITY DISHES HAVE DETECTED TRACES MOSTLY ON THE EAST SIDE OF THE ISLAND.
What KIND of radioactivity is it?

WELL, I'VE ANALYZED THE ENERGY SIGNATURE OF THE RADIATION, AND...
...IT APPEARS TO BE A METALLIC ELEMENT, LIKE URANIUM.
92
U
238.

WE'D NARROWED THE POSSIBILITIES DOWN TO TSU-BLOCK, SOLITARY CONFINEMENT, AND PROTECTIVE CUSTODY.
BUT NOW IT APPEARS THERE ARE TRACES REPORTED IN THE GENERAL POPULATION, AROUND WA-BLOCK AND THEREABOUTS.

WE'RE CURRENTLY CROSS-REFERENCING THE MOVEMENTS OF VARIOUS INMATES IN ORDER TO PIN IT DOWN.
GREAT. Thanks, Keiko. Moving ON...

OKAY, item FOUR: CLEANLINESS. I'm hearing back about a lot of inmates that are refusing to go to the WATERFALLS to shower. Word's gotten AROUND about some unfortunate INCIDENTS in th--
uh...
...GUPTA? Something on your MIND?

HUH?
ME? No, sorry. NOTHING, Boss-man. I mean...
...other than launching HALF the smelly cloakers into the SUN and the rest into a BLACK HOLE, I got no SOLUTIONS.

HA HA HA HA HA HA HA HA HA HA HA HA HA HA HA HA HA
All right, all right. Enough of THAT.
I'm going to be looking to ALL of you for solutions for this SHOWER situation, GOT it?
In the MEAN-TIME, you're DISMISSED.

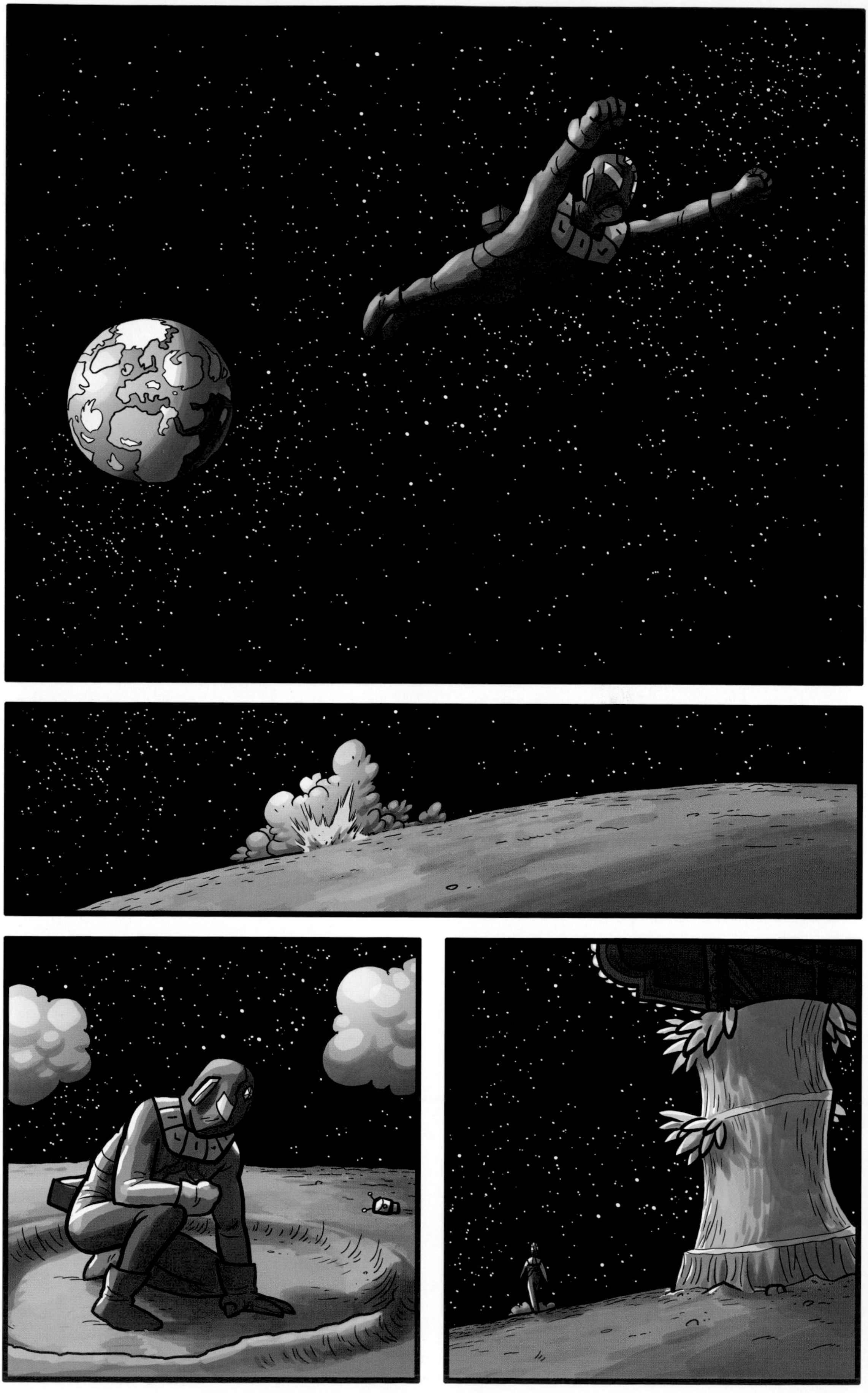

CRYSTAL EMPIRE CASINO

GORDY. HOW GOES IT? EVERYTHING GOOD?
WELL ENOUGH, MR. GUPTA. NOW, BEFORE YOU SIT DOWN...
...I GOT TO TELL YOU YOU'RE NOT GOING TO BE PLAYING HERE UNTIL YOU SETTLE YOUR TAB WITH THE HOUSE.

I KNOW THAT. WHAT DO YOU THINK I GOT IN HERE, MY ULTRA-LAUNDRY?
HEY. SOUNDS GOOD. JUST PASSING ON WHAT I'VE BEEN TOLD.
THE MADAME WILL SEE YOU IN A FEW MINUTES IF YOU WANT TO GO WAIT IN THE PARLOR.

LADY, I GOT A **SCHEDULE** TO KEEP HERE...

ALL **RIGHT** THEN.
FINALLY.

YES, MR. GUPTA. I QUITE **AGREE**.
FINALLY.

FINALLY YOU'VE BROUGHT ME WHAT YOU **OWE** ME.
YOU ARE **LATE** THIS MONTH. THAT IS BAD **BUSINESS**.
AND YOU ARE A **BUSINESSMAN**, ARE YOU NOT? IN THE BUSINESS OF MAKING SURE MY **PRINCE** IS SAFE IN YOUR LITTLE **CAGE** DOWN THERE?

WELL, I-- LOOK, THIS STUFF IS HARD TO CONVERT FROM THE LOCAL MONEY. I GOTTA GO ALL THE WAY TO THE NEBULA OF THE ETERNAL SUNRISE TO GET MORE THAN A COUPLE BARS.
MAYBE YOU CAN TAKE PAYMENT IN SOMETHING OTHER THAN SUPERNOVA GOLD. SOME ORGANISM IMITATOR MINERALS, MAYBE, OR--
YES, YES.

VERY BORING.
TAKE-GON, PLEASE RELIEVE HIM OF HIS BURDEN.

HUNGGH. LIGHT.
TOO LIGHT.
OKAY, NOW WAIT, THAT'S ANOTHER THING.
I'M WORKING ON SOMETHING THAT'S GOING TO TAKE A LITTLE WHILE, SO UH...

SO NEXT MONTH, I CAN GET YOU THE REST OF THIS PAYMENT, PLUS NEXT MONTH'S PAYMENT, PLUS A LITTLE BONUS TO--
MM-HM.

WHOA -- WAIT! WAIT!!
STOP! WHAT ARE YOU DOING??
YES, RIGHT. OKAY.
PERHAPS THERE ARE A FEW THINGS I HAVE NOT MADE CLEAR.

NO, WAIT! WAIT!! VICTORIA PLEASE!! HOLD ON!!
WE HAVE EXTENDED YOU SOME CREDIT.
WITH CREDIT COMES OBLIGATION. WE MUST ALL UPHOLD OUR VOWS, CORRECT?
HITOTSU! YOU MUST NEVER COME TO THE MOON WITH AN EMPTY CONTAINER.

VICTORIA! PLEASE! GIVE ME A SECOND!
IF YOU DO SUCH A THING, THEN YOU CANNOT EXPECT US TO UPHOLD OUR VOWS EITHER.
HITOTSU! TRY NOT TO CUT OFF A WORTHLESS SCUMBAG'S ARM!

NO!! NO!! VICTORIAAA!!

HAHAHAHAHA
OH, MR. GUPTA.
DO NOT WORRY.

YOU ARE USEFUL TO US.
YOU ARE WELL-POSITIONED. MORALLY FLEXIBLE.
THESE ARE THINGS THAT OUR LITTLE PRINCE NEEDS IN HIS TIME DOWN THERE WITH THE LESSER SPECIES.

WE WOULD BE FOOLISH TO EXPECT YOU TO BE ABLE TO DO YOUR WORK DOWN THERE AT 50% CAPACITY.
RIGHT, RIGHT!
YOU WON'T REGRET THIS, YOU REALLY WO--
BUT YOU KNOW, ACTUALLY...

...I'M SURE 90% WILL BE FINE.
WHAT? NO--
N--

"AND THEN YOU CAN'T HEAR NOTHIN', HUH?"

NAH. EVERY TIME HE TAKE ONE OF THESE LITTLE 'NILLAS UNDER HIS WING, THEY JUST SIT THERE.
FOR HOURS. BARELY MOVE. BARELY MAKE A SOUND.
WHAT, SO LIKE, NOTHIN' HAPPENS AT ALL, ESE?

WELL, HE'LL FLINCH EVERY ONCE IN A WHILE, MAYBE ANSWER A QUESTION NO ONE ELSE HEARS.
CRAP LIKE THAT.

SO, LIKE A RIGHT HAND MON KINDA THING?
HA. HELL NO. I MEAN, HE'S TELLIN' 'EM SECRET STUFF, ALL RIGHT.
BUT YOU WOULD NOT WANT THAT, BROTHER.

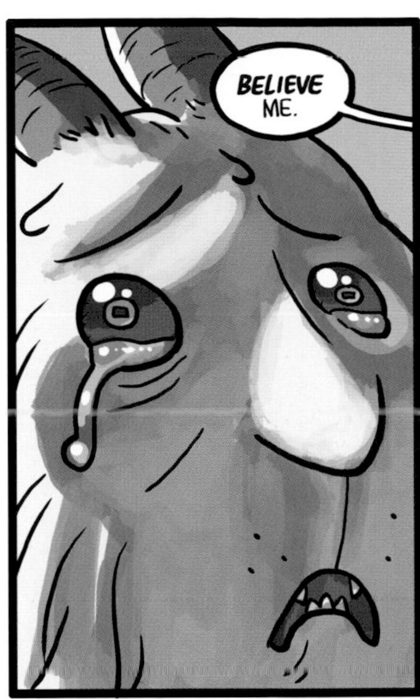
BELIEVE ME.

CHECK-IN
GUPTA
AJIT

NNF

What the HELL...

THOO

THOOM THOOM

CENTRAL! This is CHAU! We need BACKUP in KAI-BLOCK! We got another RAMPAGE going on RIGHT NOW!!
TH

THOOM

He's going to start a damned **SPECIES RIOT**--
SHING
Get the **WARDEN!** And clear out all the inmates you can--
SHING
And tell **DR. ZHANG** to get **READY**-- there are going to be **CASUALTIES** in about thirty **SECON**--

FSHH

HNNGH
HEY BUDDY.
GET AWAY FROM ME, GUPTA. GET OUT OF MY GOJ-DAMNED WAY.

COME WITH ME. STEP ASIDE FOR JUST A SECOND. YOU DON'T WANT THIS.
YOU DON'T KNOW WHAT I REDKING WANT. GET YOUR HANDS OFF OF ME!
HEY. HEY.

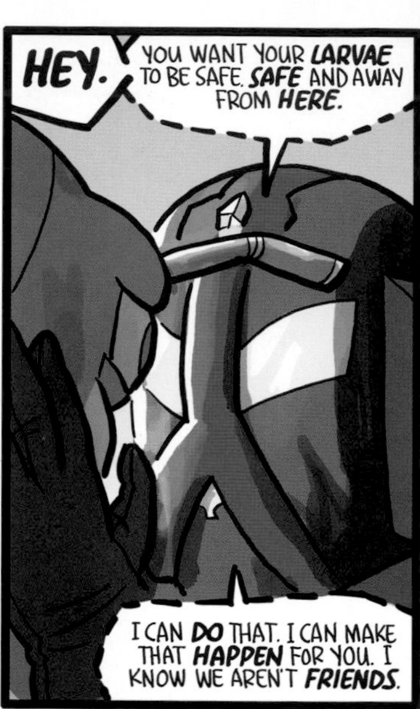
HEY.
YOU WANT YOUR LARVAE TO BE SAFE. SAFE AND AWAY FROM HERE.
I CAN DO THAT. I CAN MAKE THAT HAPPEN FOR YOU. I KNOW WE AREN'T FRIENDS.

LIFE AIN'T FAIR. NOT FOR ANY LIZZA IN HERE. BUT GOOD THINGS CAN HAPPEN.
YOU AND ME-- WE JUST NEED TO COME TO A LITTLE ARRANGEMENT.

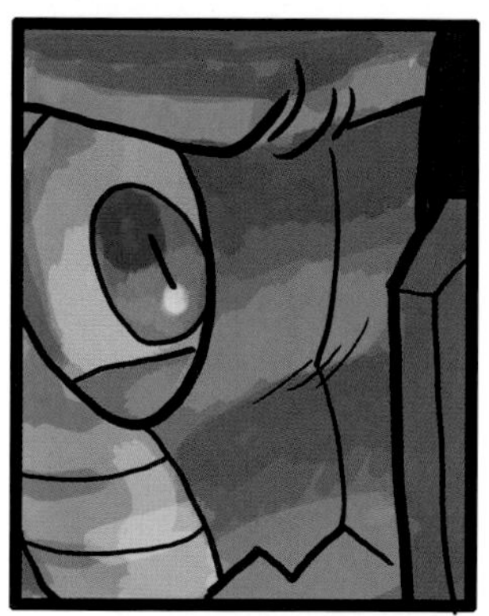

DAD

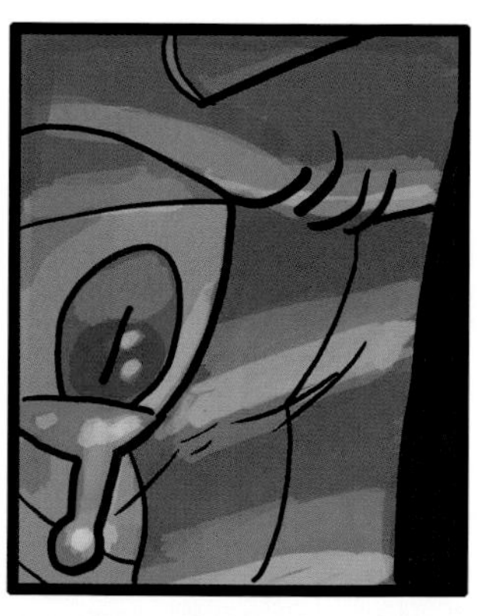

OKAY!
IT'S ALL RIGHT! EVERYTHING'S OKAY!

EXCUSE ME, MADAME.

YOU HAVE A CALL. IT'S MR. GUPTA.

THIS HAD BETTER BE GOOD.

Oh, it IS.
It's good for ME, it's good for YOU. I'll tell ya what, Victoria, it's damn good for EVERYBODY.
Something to close the GAP between us.

Got a new CONNECT. And this one's EASY. PREDICT-ABLE. No RADIO DART whisperin' in his ear, makin' DECISIONS for him.
I got him under my THUMB.
I DON'T CARE WHERE YOU GET THE MONEY.
LET THE LIZZERS AND THE SECRET ANIMALS HAVE THEIR POISON. BUT IT STAYS OUT OF MY SON.

Roger THAT.
Okay, I gotta GO.
Be talking to you SOON.

EMPLOYEE OF THE MONTH
AJIT GUPTA
EPTEMBER
BYE.

episode

3

怪獣マックス

WHOOFY™

MY STYLE IS MANIC, MY FLOW'S VOLCANIC, WE IN YOUR TOWN, FOOL, IT'S TIME TO PANIC.
MY CREW ROLLS DEEP-- TWENTY THOUSAND FATHOMS-- SWATTIN' DOWN EVERY SINGLE FOKKER COMIN' AT 'EM--

GETTIN' ALL CRAZY WITH THE FLAMES I'M HUFFIN'-- 50-TON NUCLEAR FLASKS LIKE IT'S NOTHIN'--
I SAID: FOOL, IF YOU HENSHIN, I FORGOT TO MENTION-- I'LL STILL BE STOMPIN' ON BUILD-INGS WHEN YOU'RE DRAWIN' A PENSION.
YEAH!

THOUSAND TONS A' RED STEEL, YOU TWO LOOK LIKE A CLOWN-- AIN'T NO GOJ-DAMN ROBOT GONNA TAKE ME DOWN.
SLIDE IN ON MY TAIL, KICK YOU IN THE CHESTPLATE. NUCLEAR BREATH, MELT YOU DOWN WITH YOUR BEST MATE.
MY BROTHER!
CRUSHIN' IS WHAT MY ZILLAS ARE MEANT FOR. YO, CAN I GET A DISTRESS FREQ TEN-FOUR?

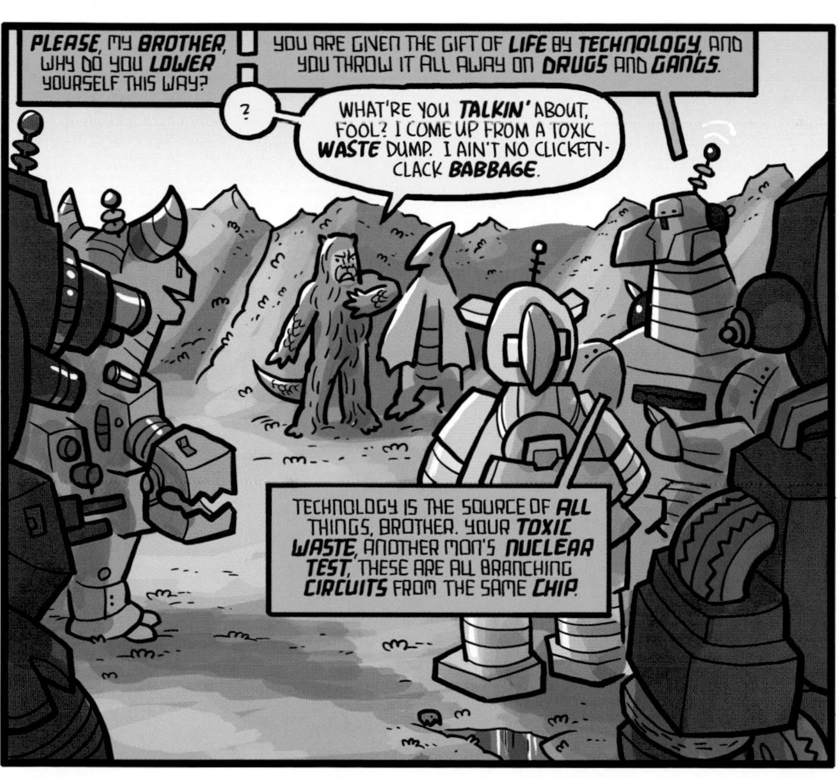
PLEASE, MY BROTHER, WHY DO YOU LOWER YOURSELF THIS WAY?
YOU ARE GIVEN THE GIFT OF LIFE BY TECHNOLOGY, AND YOU THROW IT ALL AWAY ON DRUGS AND GANGS.
?
WHAT'RE YOU TALKIN' ABOUT, FOOL? I COME UP FROM A TOXIC WASTE DUMP. I AIN'T NO CLICKETY-CLACK BABBAGE.
TECHNOLOGY IS THE SOURCE OF ALL THINGS, BROTHER. YOUR TOXIC WASTE, ANOTHER MON'S NUCLEAR TEST, THESE ARE ALL BRANCHING CIRCUITS FROM THE SAME CHIP.

AND THIS SO-CALLED 'MONSTA LIFE'--THIS IS WHAT THE MAN WANTS OF YOU, SO HE CAN PUT YOU IN A CATEGORY, MY BROTHERS. WE ARE MORE THAN THAT. WE CAN USE THAT TECHNOLOGY TO MAKE OURSELVES MORE THAN THAT.
TIME SPENT IN PEACEFUL INTERFACE WITH THE CLOUD CAN SHOW YOU THAT--
PEDDLE THAT TECHNO-BABBLE ELSEWHERE, HOLY ROLLER. WE AIN'T BUYIN'.

HA! YEAH, INTERFACE THIS, TIN MON!
HA HA!
AS YOU LIKE, MY FRIENDS. PC BE WITH YOU.
NOW, MY BROTHERS. HEED THIS: THESE ARE OUR WORST SELVES. WE IGNORE THEM --AS WELL AS OUR OPPRESSORS-- AT OUR PERIL.
THE MAN MAY HOLD US DOWN, BUT IT IS OUR BASE, ANIMALISTIC NATURE THAT CAN HOLD US BACK.
LOSE SIGHT OF THE LOGIC OF THE CLOUD FOR EVEN A MOMENT...

...AND WE MAY BETRAY OUR MOST CHERISHED **BELIEFS**.

NO SUCH THING as a HALFWAY MONSTA

ALL RIGHT. THIS URANIUM'S LOOKING **GOOD**. THE **COLOR'S** WEIRD, BUT THE **SPECTROMETER** SAYS IT'LL GET LIZZAS HIGH AS **ANYTHING**.
GREAT. WELL, AS MUCH AS I'VE **ENJOYED** THIS, HAVE YOU MADE ANY PROGRESS FINDING MY **KIDS**?

TAKE IT **EASY**, INMATE. THAT AIN'T THE WAY IT **WORKS**. I GOT STUFF TO DO AROUND HERE.
WE MADE A REDKING **DEAL**, MAN! **I** CAME THROUGH. YOU CAN'T JUST--

LISTEN. THIS HERE'S THE **JUNGLE**, BABY.
YOU GOT **NO POWER**, BUT THIS IS A DEAL THAT COULD WORK OUT **OKAY** FOR YOU IF I WANT IT TO. SO LET ME GIVE YOU SOME **ADVICE**:

"...WHY DON'T YOU JUST STICK TO TELLING ME WHAT I WANT TO HEAR."
WE ARE THE CHOSEN ONES, MY BROTHERS.
CHOSEN BY THE CLOUD TO ENLIGHTEN OUR LESS FORTUNATE PEERS ABOUT WHAT CAN AWAIT THEM IF THEY FOLLOW US.

A WORLD OF REASON. A WORLD OF MATHEMATICAL PEACE. AND THIS IS WHY THE ENLIGHTENED SANCTUM OF OUR CELLBLOCK K1 IS THE ENVY OF ALL OF KAIJUMAX.
IF OUR BRETHREN COULD ONLY BE MADE TO UNDERSTAND, THEN--
Hey MECHA-ZON!

You got a VISITOR. Head on OVER.

WHO IS IT?
NOW IS NOT A GOOD TIME, OPPRESSOR. MY FOLLOWERS AND I ARE--
NOW'S when it's HAPPENING, fella. Use it or LOSE it.
SIGH
MY BROTHERS, WE WILL HAVE TO CONTINUE THIS LATER IN THE DAY.

THIS MAN, CONSTRUCTED OF MEAT AND ANGER, HAS NO RESPECT FOR OUR TIME.
YAWN Hey, friend.
Trees and BOULDERS will break my SHOULDERS...

"...but WORDS will never hurt me."
Yes, Ma'am, I UNDERSTAND. Most CERTAINLY.
You've made yourself VERY clear.

You wanted to **SEE** me, Warden?

Then I don't see what the **PROBLEM** is, Kang. It's a simple **OUT-AND-BACK ASSIGNMENT.**

That's just **IT**, Ma'am. What you're **TALKING** about falls under the jurisdiction of Team **G.R.E.A.T.**, not **US**. If it's so **SIMPLE**, why not leave it to **THEM**?

I mean, I **KNOW** it's just a short **HOP**, but the only guards I've **GOT** are coming off a **SHIFT**. They're **TIRED**.

NO, BOSS, NO. THAT'S NOT WHAT I'M SAYING.

IT'S JUST -- THESE ATTEMPTS ON YOUR LIFE -- MAYBE WE NEED TO GET YOU SOME-WHERE A LITTLE SAFER UNTIL THE HEAT IS OFF.

PROTECTIVE CUSTODY, MAYBE.

NO, WHOOFY, STOP THAT. GET OUT OF THERE.

ENOUGH.

YOU THINK IT WOULD BE BETTER FOR ME TO JUST HIDE AWAY FROM THESE THREATS. FOR THE BOSS TO HIDE IN... IN SOME TINY CAPSULE.

GURM.

LIKE THOSE PRETENDERS TO THE THRONE IN HIROSHIMA.

NO, BOSS, NO. IT DOESN'T SOUND GOOD, BUT AH, I MEAN, I-IF YOU'RE DEAD...
I-I MEAN, YOU DYING IS SOMETHING WE JUST CAN'T RISK.
GOB.

sigh
THE PROBLEM OF MY SUCCESSION IS SOMETHING I'M DEALING WITH.
GOJ. HOW MY DNA FELL INTO THAT VOLCANO AND CREATED THIS, I'LL NEVER KNOW.
LURP.

RIGHT, BOSS, SO WE GOTTA THINK ABOUT YOUR SAFETY. THE CRYPS HAVE BEEN FLAME-BREATHIN' FOR YA SINCE SHOWA TIMES...
...AND YOU KNOW THE DON AIN'T PLEASED WITH HOW YOU TURNED DOWN HIS PEACE OFFERING.
GUBZ!

HIM AND HIS CREW-- THESE YOUNG HOTSHOTS FRESH OUT OF THE BALL, THEY'RE JUST DYIN' FOR A WAY TO PROVE THEMSELVES.
KNOCKIN' OFF THE BOSS WOULD SHOW THEY AIN'T JUST SOME BABY EVOLUTION, Y'KNOW?
GET THAT OUT OF MY FACE, Y'STUPID AMBERGRIS.

HEY, AWAKEN UP BACK THERE! IT'S GOJ-DAMN LUNCHTIME!
ALL RIGHT, I'M COMIN', MON.
KORUGON-- YOU SPEAK SENSE, I KNOW THIS.
BUT TO BURY MY FACE IN THE SAND LIKE SOME CONE-HEADED 'BORA? WHILE OUR ENEMIES PARADE AROUND PROUDLY?
IT WOULD BE LIKE 2004 ALL OVER AGAIN. THE EMPTY DECADE. NO ONE WANTS THAT.

面目が潰れてしまうっ
WE WOULD LOSE FACE.
WE HAVE LOOMED SO LARGE, EARNED SO MUCH RESPECT FOR SO MANY YEARS, AND NOW ALL THESE ZILLAS WOULD JUST SEE US AS...
AS...
'EY DAD!
DAD!!

GLUBZ!!
WHAT THE--??

GOJ DAMN IT, WHOOFY! YOU'RE LIKE A METEOR-ITE AROUND MY NECK!! YOU'RE PULLING ME TO THE BOTTOM OF THE SEA!

YOU WERE WORTHLESS **THEN**-- YOU COULDN'T EVEN GET OUT OF YOUR OWN **EGG**-
AND YOU'RE **GOJ-DAMN** WORTHLESS **NOW!**

GET **OUT!** GET OUT OF MY REDKING **SIGHT!**
GWAAH!

BOSS, ARE YOU **SURE** YOU WANT TO DO TH--
SHUT UP.

EH HUH HUH HUUUH.
snerk
GUUH HUH HUH HUH **HUUUH.**
snerk snerk
HEY.

HEY, **YOU**.
YOU WANNA **PLAY**?

HWHUH?
H-HOW YOU GET **IN** HERE?
ME? I **DREAMED** MY WAY TO THIS PLACE.
DOES IT **MATTER**?
SO, DO YOU **WANNA**?

I-I NOT SURE IF I CAN--
B-BUT THAT SOUND **FUN**.
M-MAYBE...

M-MAYBE I ASK MY **DAD** IF I--
?
WHUH?
WHERE--

"WHERE HE **GO?**"
So.
You finally show **UP**.

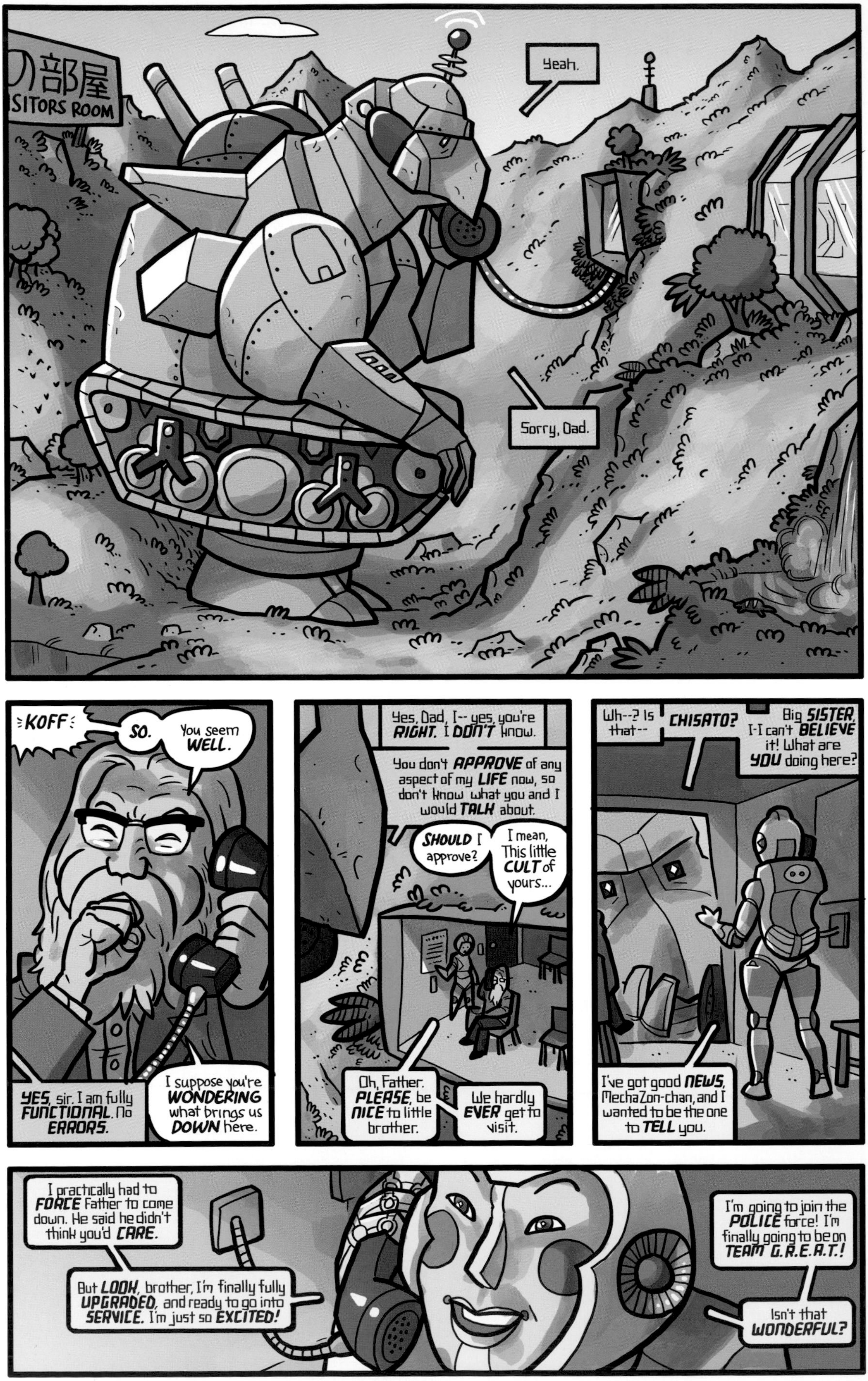

の部屋
SITORS ROOM
Yeah.
Sorry, Dad.

uh... Team G.R.E.A.T.?
Well, I -- I mean, that IS certainly big NEWS. But I mean...

What's the MATTER, brother? Don't you think I can HACK it?
I can DEADLIFT 40 tons of STEEL, and my TARGETING COMPUTER is accurate down to THREE CENTIMETERS.
Why, my new LEG-TURBINES are TOP-OF-THE-LINE. Father and GORD worked on them for SEVEN MONTHS, just to push them over the SOUND BARRIER.
I've got a new detachable STEERING COLUMN that jacks into my SHOULDERS.
Father says that there's even a chance Admiral FURUYA will pilot me.

'PILOT you?' But--
I mean NO, it's not any of THAT, Chi-chan. I--I KNOW you can DO it.
It's just--
The SYSTEM you'd serve-- it holds DOWN our people. Don't you--
BAH! The "SYSTEM".

Typical LEAKING HEART response. Perhaps you don't realize what's BECOME of Nagoya since you failed to DEFEND it.
Crime is RAMPANT. The prefecture has declared it a MONSTER LAWLESS ZONE.
CHISATO is finally doing what you WOULDN'T, despite ALL your GIFTS.
And I know SHE won't turn on her BENEFACTORS and fail to ACT when the chips are DOWN.

Dad, I'm not going to have this ARGUMENT.
You KNOW I've RENOUNCED violence.
And it's like I've TOLD you--I realized I have no ANGER against the monsters in here. The SYSTEM has been stacked AGAINST them since the day they were SPAWNED.

The one we created you to DESTROY-- he wasn't MISUNDERSTOOD. He was a THUG and a KILLER.
I DEFY you to look in my face, and in CHISATO'S face--knowing EVERYTHING that came AFTER--
...and TELL us that you shouldn't have KILLED him when you had the CHANCE.

Father, I... DO wish things would have turned out DIFFERENTLY.
But devotion to the CLOUD and to NON-VIOLENCE are no trivial MATTER.
They are my most cherished BELIEFS.

"And no one can say I haven't **SUFFERED** for them."
DRINK
LAGER

BOY, this NEIGHBOR-HOOD has seen better DAYS.
HA! Yeah, in the PALEOZOIC era, maybe.

Hell, where do you THINK these inbred SHARK-SHAGGERS are going to set up their little LABS? Nice quiet island, no CRUISERS happening by...
Heh heh.
Nice place to raise a BROOD of half-wit ZOOKIES...

HA HA!
AHEM DISPATCH, this is JEONG. We're pulling UP. Looks QUIET.
ACKNOWLEDGED. PROCEED WITH CAUTION.
YOU ARE NOT EXPECTED TO RUN INTO ANY RESISTANCE, BUT...
...but who KNOWS what these SCALY-NECKS have got stashed AWAY, huh?

Huntin' and trappin' CASSOWARIES and COELACANTH 'round here, they gotta be loaded for a FIGHT. YEE-HAW!
ALL RIGHT. REPORT IN WHEN YOU HAVE THE SUSPECT OR SUSPECTS IN CUS-TODY. KEIKO OUT.
Heh heh.

Okay, GUPTA. Looks like everything's through that PASS over there.
You READY? Got everything?

Sure DO. All I need are the AUTHORITY and the SHIELD.
Let's take these volcano-billies DOWN.

Be CAREFUL in there. Watch the CORNERS.
SHING
SHING
Yeah, yeah. READY?

YEAH.
Let's GO.

HHNNGHPH

HNNG

HEY--

FREEZE--
FREEZE!!

VASSH

OH NO.

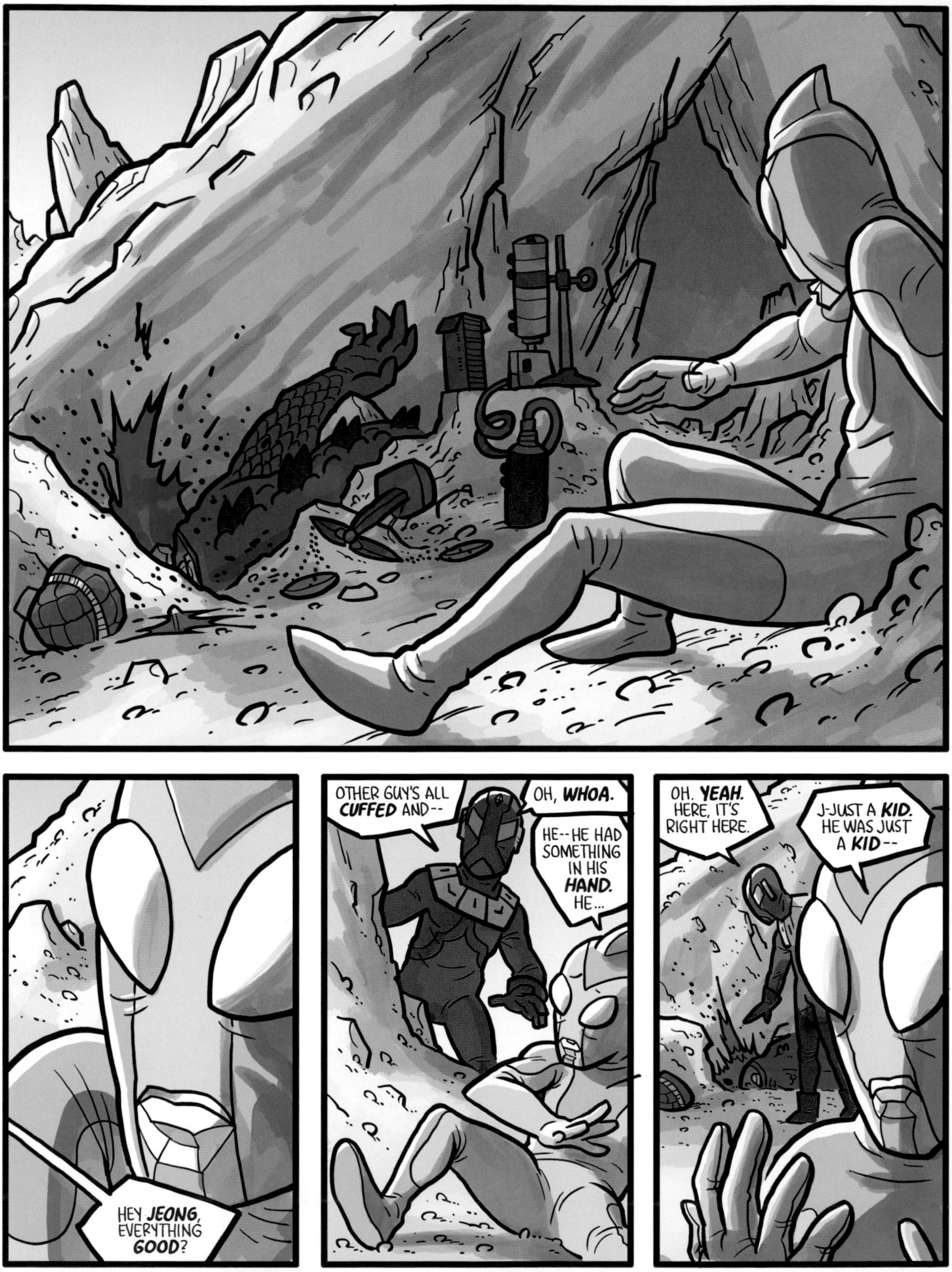

HEY **JEONG**, EVERYTHING **GOOD**?

OTHER GUY'S ALL **CUFFED** AND--
OH, **WHOA.**
HE--HE HAD SOMETHING IN HIS **HAND.** HE...

OH. **YEAH.** HERE, IT'S RIGHT HERE.
J-JUST A **KID.** HE WAS JUST A **KID**--

YEAH. CHECK THIS **OUT.** LOOKS LIKE SOME KIND OF **COMMUNICATOR.**
MAKETO
C-**COMMUNICATOR**?

YEAH, IT'S A SURE BET THAT HE'S WORKING WITH THE DON DOWN IN HIROSHIMA.
NICE WORK FINDING THAT.
"HEY MON, YOU DOING OKAY?"

ME? SURE, I GUESS. WHAT'S UP?
YEAH. GOOD. I-I MEAN, NOTHIN'.
LOOK, I DON'T KNOW IF YOU KNOW THIS, BUT uh...
I'M CHANGIN' CRATERS. I uh, I'M GONNA GO OVER TO TSU BLOCK.

OVER TO WHERE THE CRYPTIDS ARE. THEY SAID I COULD JOIN 'EM THERE.
YEAH?

YEAH. WE'RE NOT GONNA BE CRATER-MATES NO MORE, MON. Y'KNOW? I, uh, I GOTTA GET WITH MY CORNER. THE ONES THAT GOT MY BACK.
HUFF
C'MON. THAT'S A LOAD OF CRAP. THEY DON'T GOT YOUR BACK. YOU AIN'T WORTH A RAI-STONE TO THEM.
SOON AS THEY'RE DONE WITH YOU, THEY'RE GONNA DROP YOU LIKE A CHEWED F-16.

sniff
WELL, WHAT WOULD YOU HAVE ME DO, CLOAKER?! THEY OWN ME.
THEY PUT THEIR BRAND ON ME.
I KNOW THEY DON'T CARE, BUT IF I DON'T ISLAND UP WITH SOMEONE, I'M JUST A MINYA-ASS TARGET TO EVERY MEGAFAUNA UP IN THIS REDKING PLACE!!

...SORRY.
YOU'RE RIGHT. IT'S NONE OF MY BUSINESS.
sniff

Y-YOU KNOW...
NOT THAT I EVER SAW HIM MUCH GROWIN' UP, BUT MY DAD ALWAYS SAID WE MAKE OUR OWN LUCK.
AND IF SOMETHIN' BAD HAPPENED TO YOU, WELL, THAT WAS JUST YOUR OWN FAULT.

THE THING THEY GOT ME ON, IT WAS KIND OF LIKE THAT.
COUPLE COMES OUT TO DEVIL'S CREEK. GETS SPOOKED.
EVERY SINGLE PATH AWAY FROM ME LEADS OUT OF THE WOODS.

EVERY PATH EXCEPT ONE.
JUST BAD LUCK.

BUT IT WASN'T THEIR BAD LUCK.
IT WAS MINE. I PUSH IT ON PEOPLE. I GOT MORE THAN ENOUGH TO GO AROUND.

IN MY LIFE, EVERY TIME IT COULDA GONE ONE WAY OR THE OTHER, IT WENT BAD.
GROWIN' UP IN THOSE DAMN WOODS. MY PARENTS FIGHTING WHENEVER MY DAD CAME AROUND.
HELL, I NEVER EVEN HAD A CHANCE.

YEAH, WELL.
AIN'T THAT WHAT LIFE IS?

EVERY DAY'S JUST ABOUT ROLLING THEM BONES.
HOPING FOR BOXCARS, BUT DEALIN' WITH WHAT LIFE SENDS YA.

YEAH, I KNOW.
I KNOW.
IT'S JUST THAT FOR ME...

"...THEY'RE ALWAYS COMIN' UP SNAKE EYES."

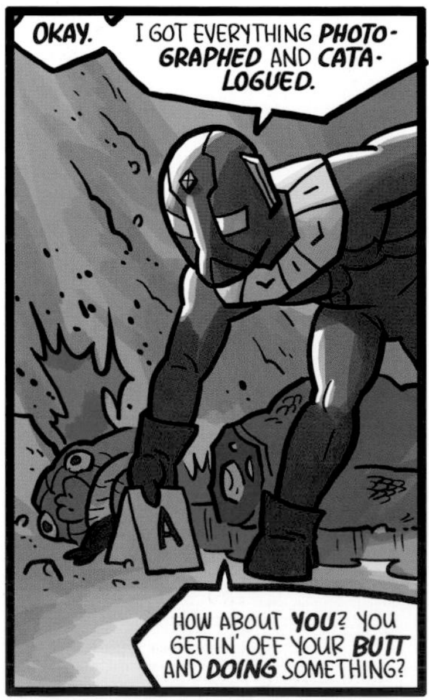
OKAY.
I GOT EVERYTHING PHOTO-GRAPHED AND CATA-LOGUED.
HOW ABOUT YOU? YOU GETTIN' OFF YOUR BUTT AND DOING SOMETHING?

HUAARCH
OH, JEEZ...

COME ON, MAN, WE GOTTA HOOK THIS OTHER GUY UP AND GET GOIN'.
PULL IT TOGETHER.
ptoo

All right. You GOOD? I'm calling this IN.
You're looking a little green around the GILLS.
I'm OK.

KEIKO, this is GUPTA.
We got the suspect in CUSTODY. He's CUFFED and FRISKED-- we're towing him back to K·MAX.
OUR INTEL SAID TWO SUSPECTS. WHAT HAPPENED TO THE OTHER ONE?

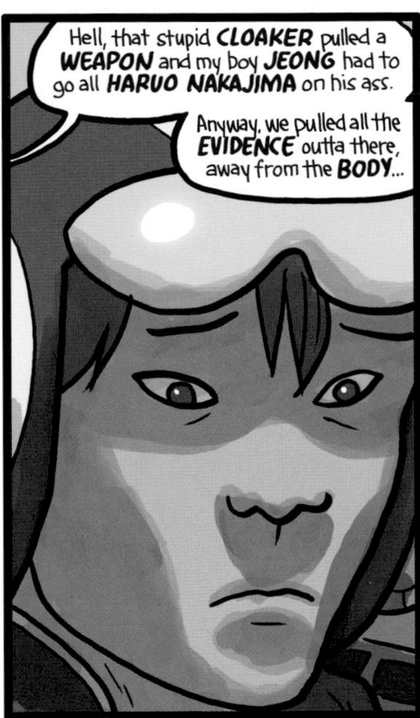
Hell, that stupid CLOAKER pulled a WEAPON and my boy JEONG had to go all HARUO NAKAJIMA on his ass.
Anyway, we pulled all the EVIDENCE outta there, away from the BODY...

"...that piece of crap's probably EXPLODING right about NOW."
HEY PREACHER-MON! GOT AN ELECTRO-SERMON FOR ME?
YO RUSTY! 'JA HEAD IN FOR AN OIL CHANGE?
WHAT'S A MATTER? YOUR PILOT ASLEEP IN THERE?

EYE DRILL #2
GUT ACCELERATOR
CHARGING 71%
HEY, YA GOT A LITTLE SOMETHING ON THE BACK 'A YER HEAD--
I THINK IT'S A HOVERCRAFT!
VOICE PRINT: NEGATIVE
HA HA HA!
VOICE PRINT: NEGATIVE
TRIPLE ZERO
11% MATCH
20% MATCH
32% MATCH
40% MATCH
GRAVITY UZI
THE BIG HAND
INDEX ROCKET
MIDDLE CHAINGUN
RING MASER
PINKIE KNIFE
PLASMA HIP SHOT
CHEST'Q'RAY
WEAPON LOCK
SPRING LOADED KNIFE
LOADING
DUAL ARC LASER POD
VIOLET WAVE

HEY, YA RUST HURRICANE. KEEP IT MOVIN'.

HOLY ADMIN, ARE YOU WELL? YOU LOOK AS IF THE MEAT CREATURES HAVE--

NO. I AM FINE, BROTHER FOGRUEDA.
I AM FINE.
TSS
THE CLOUD IS A JUST MISTRESS, AND WITH HER LIES ALL SALVATION.

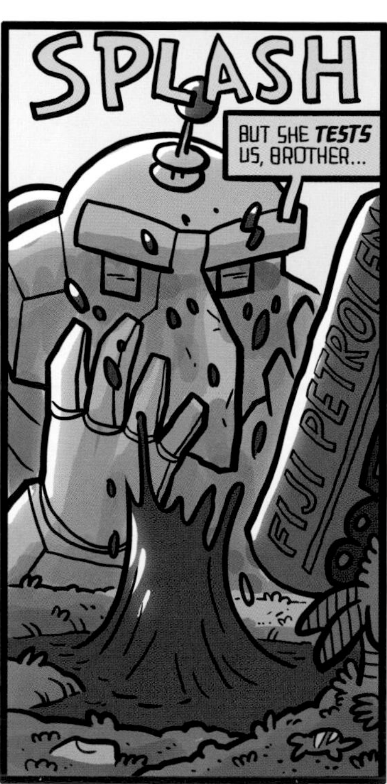
SPLASH
BUT SHE TESTS US, BROTHER...

"...SHE SURELY TESTS US."
INCOMING CALL
MATSUMOTO
Hm?

Dr. MATSUMOTO? HELLO, Ma'am. Er... this is my PERSONAL phone.
I'm in the OFFICE. You can call me on the OFFICE PHONE if--
Yes, well, it will just be a MOMENT.
You have a certain PRISONER coming in today.

Yes, that's RIGHT, Ma'am. I believe he's coming in right NOW. Is there--
This PRISONER has ALLIED himself with certain dangerous INDIVIDUALS and has been PRIVY to a great deal of SENSITIVE INFORMATION over the years.
As such, he is the LINCHPIN of the state's CASE against the DON and the MAKETO gang in HIROSHIMA.

YES, ma'am, I UNDERSTAND. I'll make sure he goes directly to PROTECTIVE CUSTODY and stays well out of the way of any RIVAL--
No, no, that won't be NECESSARY.
I'm told that your KI BLOCK has a reputation for being very SAFE.
I think it would be best if we just placed him THERE.

"I'm sure they'll take good CARE of him."

INTAKE

Stop on the white DOT, inmate. Welcome to KAIJUMAX. These are the RULES.

You EAT what we GIVE you. No more TOP OF THE FOOD CHAIN stuff.

You SLEEP and WAKE UP when we TELL you. Nobody's slumbering for DECADES in HERE.

You DEPOSIT WASTE when and WHERE we say. This ain't no SUPERFUND site.
JEONG! You're BACK! Hey, how'd it GO?
TSST

And LASTLY, you keep your CLAWS, TENTACLES, SCYTHES, and PSEUDOPODS to yourself. Now MOVE.
Hey, you OKAY?
JEONG? Hey, you all RIGHT?

My shift's just about UP. You want to get a DRINK, maybe over at Daisuke's PUB? We can--
!
Get your HANDS off me. Don't TALK to me.
Just l-leave me ALONE.

"THE NEW GUY AIN'T ROARIN' TO ANYONE YET, HUH?"

NAH. FROM WHAT I HEAR, HIS REP'S BEDROCK SOLID, BUT HE AIN'T BEEN IN K-MAX YET, SO HE AIN'T GOT A CREW.
HE'S FROM NAGOYA. HE'S GOTTA BE IN WITH APE-WHALE'S BOYS.

MAYBE. WHAT I WANNA KNOW IS HOW YOU GET A REP LIKE THAT BUT NEVER GET PICKED UP ON A POLITOTOMY BEEF LIKE THE REST OF US.
31% MATCH
12% MATCH
TARGETING
YEAH. MAYBE HE'LL BE RUNNING A CREW HERE BEFORE TOO LONG.
AW, HERE HE COMES--
ARC POWERING UP...

WHAT THE--

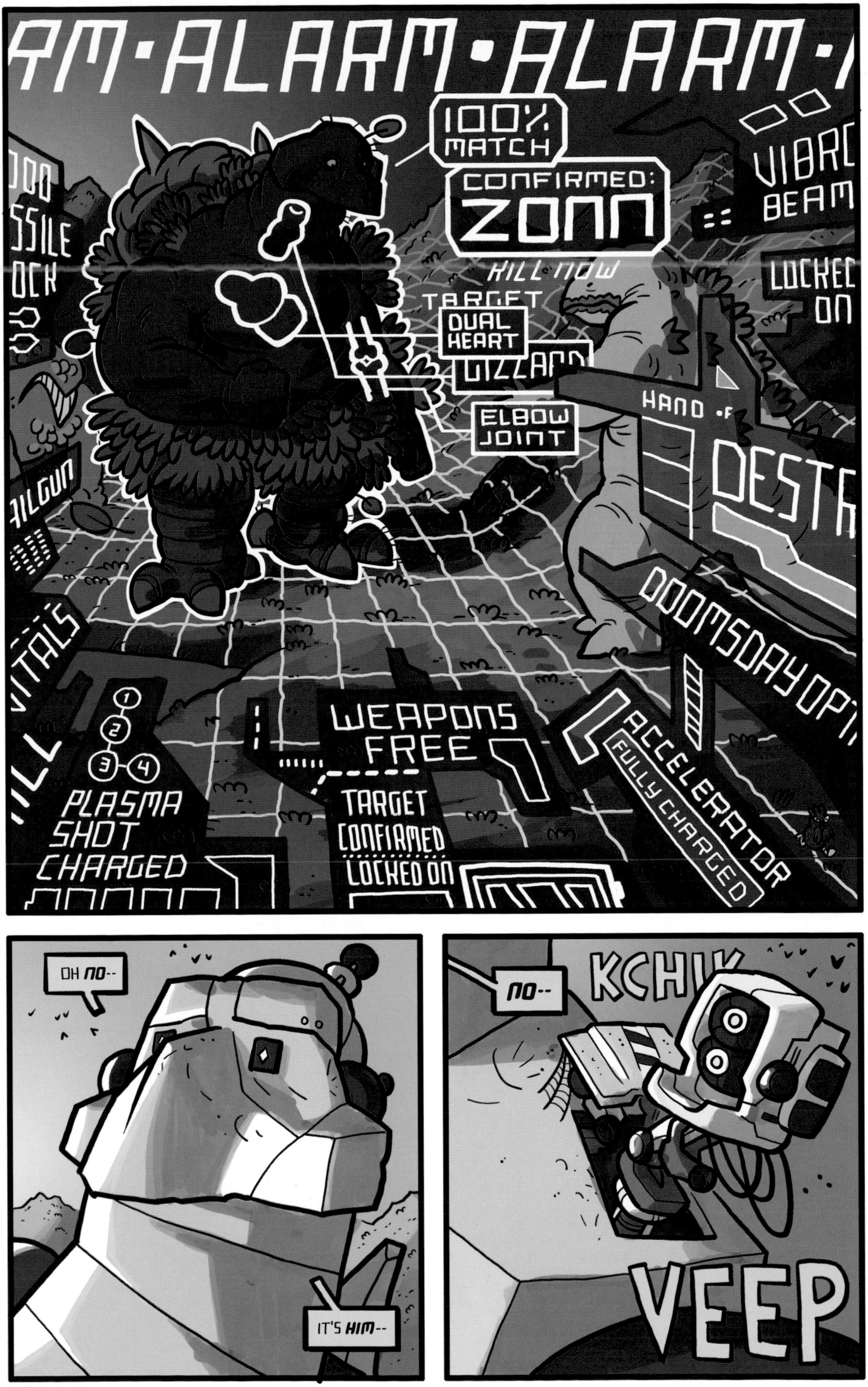

RM • ALARM • ALARM •

100% MATCH

CONFIRMED: ZONN

KILL NOW

TARGET

DUAL HEART

GIZZARD

ELBOW JOINT

VIBRO BEAM

LOCKED ON

HAND OF DESTR

DOOMSDAY OPT

VITALS

PLASMA SHOT CHARGED

WEAPONS FREE

TARGET CONFIRMED LOCKED ON

ACCELERATOR

FULLY CHARGED

NO!!
KCHAK

VEEP
STOP--
NO--
KCHAK
VEEP
CHK

AH! ZONN!
WE WERE TOLD ABOUT YOUR ARRIVAL. I AM KORUGON, AND I'M HERE TO WELCOME YOU ON BEHALF OF APE-WHALE, THE BOSS OF THE--
YO, HOLD UP A SEC, LIZZA. THERE'S SOMEONE I GOTTA ROAR AT FIRST.

HEY YO, HOLD UP, MY ZILLA. I WANNA TALK TO YOU.
YO! MECHAZON!

YO, PEACE, MY BROTHER, YOU KNOW WHAT I'M SAYIN'?
I AIN'T ABOUT FIGHTIN'.
IT'S BEEN ALL THESE YEARS, I JUST WANNA TELL YA SOMETHING QUICK. Y'KNOW, NOW THAT WE'RE NEIGHBORS AND ALL.
VEEP
KCHAK
NNF
WHAT... WHAT IS IT?

OH MY **GOD**.

MATSUMOTO, YOU **IDIOT**...

ALARM

ALARM

ERRNT

YES.
THAT'S RIGHT.

episode

4

怪獣マックス

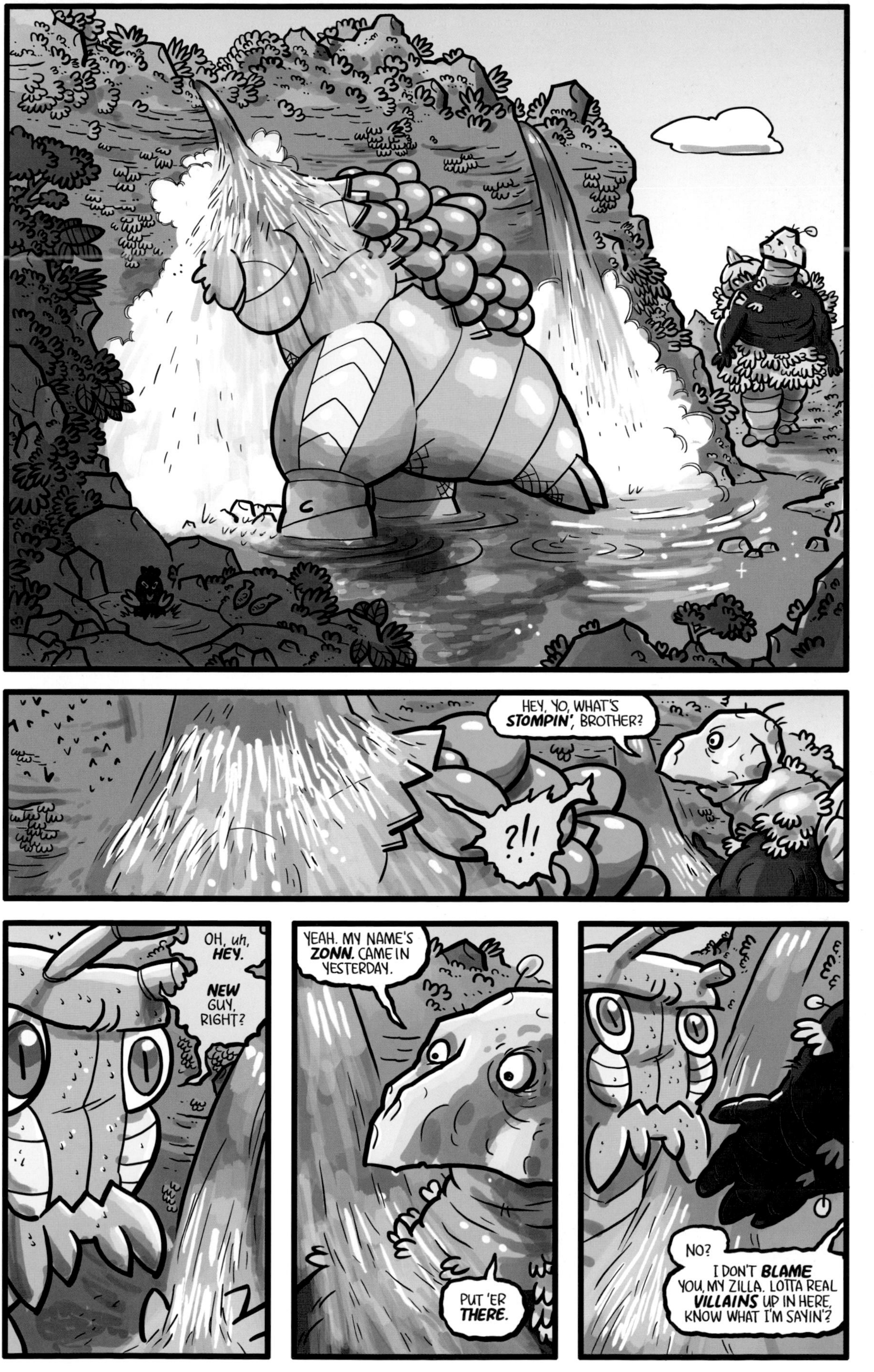

HEY, YO, WHAT'S **STOMPIN'**, BROTHER?
?!!

OH, uh, **HEY**.
NEW GUY, RIGHT?

YEAH. MY NAME'S **ZONN**. CAME IN YESTERDAY.
PUT 'ER **THERE**.

NO?
I DON'T **BLAME** YOU, MY ZILLA. LOTTA REAL **VILLAINS** UP IN HERE, KNOW WHAT I'M SAYIN'?

ANYWAY. YOU'RE COOL. I CAN SEE THAT. LIKE A MISUNDERSTOOD **HERO.** MAYBE EVEN A **PROTECTOR OF CHILDREN.**
RESPECT.

UH **HUH.**
SO *uh,* WHERE YOU **FROM,** FRIEND?

OH, **FAR** FROM HERE. **NAGOYA,** MOSTLY.
ALL **OVER,** REALLY. YOU KNOW WHAT IT'S **LIKE.** NO ONE'S LOOKIN' **OUT** FOR YOU, YOU GOTTA KEEP **CRUSHIN'** AND **RUNNIN',** ONE STEP AHEAD OF THE **SQUISHERS** IF YOU WANNA **LAST,** YOU FEEL ME?

YEAH, I **DO.** WHAT ABOUT **FAMILY?** DON'T YOU GOT ANYONE ON THE **OUTSIDE?**
ONCE I DID. LONG TIME **AGO** NOW.

THE BIG CITY CAN BE **TOUGH,** YOU KNOW, I MEAN, YOU JUST SHOW **UP,** THE **MAN'S** ALL UP IN YOUR BEAK.
AND JUST LIKE **THAT,** YOU GET INTO A LITTLE MISUNDERSTANDING WITH THE **LAW** AND **ZAP,** YOU KNOW? THE **125 mm ROUNDS** START FLYIN'.
THE **SPAM IN A CAN,** BROTHER, THEY DON'T CARE **WHO** THEY HIT.

SO **YEAH.** I HAD **FAMILY.** I HAD A WHOLE **CLUTCH.** THEY WERE WIPED OUT IN THREE **MINUTES.**
...

I-I'M SORRY. THAT **SUCKS,** MON. MY **LARVAE-MAMA,** I LOST HER THE SAME WAY.
YOU'RE MOVIN' **AROUND,** TRYIN' TO FEED THE **FAMILY,** BUT THERE'S ALWAYS JUST SO MANY **TANKS.**
JUST... SO MANY **TANKS.**

nnf
LEFT ME WITH TWO **KIDS** TO RAISE. NOW THEY'RE STILL **OUT** THERE, AND I BEEN TRYING TO GET **WORD** TO 'EM, BUT I MEAN, THIS **PRISON,** MON, FOR REAL.
YOU GOT NO IDEA WHO TO **TRUST.**
I **FEEL** YOU. THAT AMBERGRIS IS **HARD,** BUT YOU DO WHAT YOU **GOT** TO.
SOMETIMES FAMILY'S ALL WE **GOT.**

YEAH, AIN'T **THAT** THE TRUTH.
sniff

AIN'T THAT JUST GOJ'S HONEST--
?!!

KRAK

nnf
WHAT--

NO!

SHUT UP, **STUPID**. BE **STILL**.
NO! GET **OFF!** WHAT ARE YOU--

BASH

OHH, WERE YOU **CRYIN'**, CRUSTY? YOUR **LARVAE** GOT LOST?
BOO HOO--YOUR STUPID-ASS **SIDE NYMPH** GOT CAPPED BY THE **SQUISHERS**?
SHLORF
HNFF!

KKRK
BIG REDKING **DEAL**, LIZZA.
OH **YEAH**, I KNOW IT, FAMILY'S **IMPORTANT**. BUT **HEY**, IF THEY'RE **GONE**, WELL...
HNNO

...THEN I GUESS I JUST GOT TO MAKE SOME **MORE**.
NO--
NO--

SKREEE ONKONK

MUTATED OUT

YO, GUPTA! WHAT IS UP, MY SPACE FRIEND?
HUFF
YOU ARE MAKING THE ROUNDS, HUH, MY MAN? BRINGING THE GOODS AROUND? EVERYONE IS FEELING EASY?
I LIKE IT, I LIKE IT!

YOU. BEAT IT.
BUT--
YOU GOT YOUR STUFF, NOW MAKE YOURSELF EXTINCT, LIZZA.

ZLOOK. HOW ARE YOU THIS FINE MORNING? YOU'RE LOOKING CHIPPER.
OH, I AM, GUPTA. I AM FEELING SO GOOD, BUT I COULD ALWAYS FEEL BETTER, YOU KNOW, KYODAI?
HUFF
THAT IS WHERE YOU AND YOUR SHIPPING CONTAINER THERE COME IN, YOU KNOW WHAT I MEAN?

NOPE. I DON'T KNOW WHAT YOU MEAN AT ALL. THESE DRUGS ARE NOT FOR YOU. YOUR MOTHER WAS VERY CLEAR ON THAT.
YES, WELL, MOTHER ALSO SAYS SHE WAS CLEAR ON THE TERMS OF YOUR DEBT WITH US, AND YET HERE YOU ARE WITH NINE FINGERS.

LISTEN, YOU LITTLE M&M-EATING TURD, NOT ALL OF US HAVE EVERYTHING HANDED TO US ON A SILVER PLATTER.
WHY DON'T YOU AND YOUR FRIENDS JUST GO BACK TO YOUR LITTLE MAGMA MARRIOTT WHILE I EARN A LIVING, HUH?
YES, I BELIEVE I WILL.

MY FRIENDS AND I WILL GO AND ENJOY OUR LIVES WHILE YOU SCRAPE AND BOW TO THE MAN, AND TRY NOT TO THINK ABOUT HOW EASILY REPLACEABLE YOU ARE.
JUST LIKE YOUR PREDECESSOR WAS, AND JUST LIKE YOUR SUCCESSOR WILL BE.
HUFF
SEE YOU LATER, PEASANT.

HELLO?

LI'L BOY?
LI'L BOY, DO YOU WANT TO PLAY WITH ME? I CAN PLAY NOW.
DAD SAY HE DON'T CARE WHAT I DO.

HE YELL AT ME AND C-CALL ME STUPID AND TELL ME TO LEAVE HIM ALONE.
HE BIG AND SCARY WHEN HE GET MAD. HE, UM...
sniff
L-LI'L BOY, CAN YOU DREAM YOUR WAY HERE AGAIN?

HERE I AM, WHOOFY!
COMING HERE IS EASY. I CAN DO IT ANY TIME I WANT!
YAY!!

LI'L BOY, THAT MAKE ME SO EXCITED! I-I NEVER HAVE SUCH A GOOD FRIEND TO PLAY WITH. IT-- IT SEEM IMPOSSIBLE!
THAT MAKE ME SO HAPPY THAT I JUST WANT TO ROAR AND ROAR!!
OH...!
SORRY! SORRY, MAYBE THAT MAKE YOU SCARED.
OH, DON'T WORRY, WHOOFY.
I'M NOT SCARED.

WHY, I'M NOT SCARED OF ANY-THING.
ANYTHING IN THE WHOLE WORLD.
OKAY. YOU WANT TO HIDE FIRST, OR SHOULD I?

...23, 24, 26...
...27, 29, 30!
OKAY, READY OR NOT, HERE I COME!

duh na na, duh na na, nuh na na

nuh na nuh na NA nuh na, NA nuh na, NA nuh na

nuh na--
HEY, THERE YOU ARE!!

HA HA! I FOUND YOU, I FOUND YOU!!
GOOD JOB! YOU ARE SO SMART. SO MUCH SMARTER THAN YOUR DAD THINKS.
NOW LOOK AT THIS. LOOK WHAT I FOUND OVER HERE.

WHAT IS IT? CAN I SEE?
DON'T TOUCH IT!
THIS IS A LEAF FROM A PLANT CALLED "RYOTA'S IVY".
I STUDIED IT IN SCHOOL.

IT'S JUST A DUMB OL' PLANT, BUT...
THIS IS WHY YOU SHOULDN'T BE AFRAID OF YOUR DAD.

I MEAN, BECAUSE HOW SCARY CAN HE BE...
...IF SOMETHING THAT GROWS ALL OVER THIS ISLAND COULD HURT HIM?
WHY, JUST THIS MUCH WOULD MAKE HIM SICK.

A WHOLE TREE'S WORTH MIGHT EVEN KILL HIM.
SAY, NOW...

...I HAVE A GREAT IDEA FOR A GAME.

WHAT IF WE SLIPPED A LITTLE INTO HIS FOOD. YOU KNOW, JUST A LITTLE.
LIKE IF HE WAS YELLING AT YOU A LOT THAT DAY AND YOU NEEDED A BREAK FROM BEING YELLED AT.

JUST SO HE WAS A TINY BIT SICK. NOT TOO MUCH. NOT ENOUGH TO KILL HIM.

WOULDN'T THAT BE SO FUNNY??

HNGGH...
DON'T MOVE. YOU'LL HURT YOURSELF.

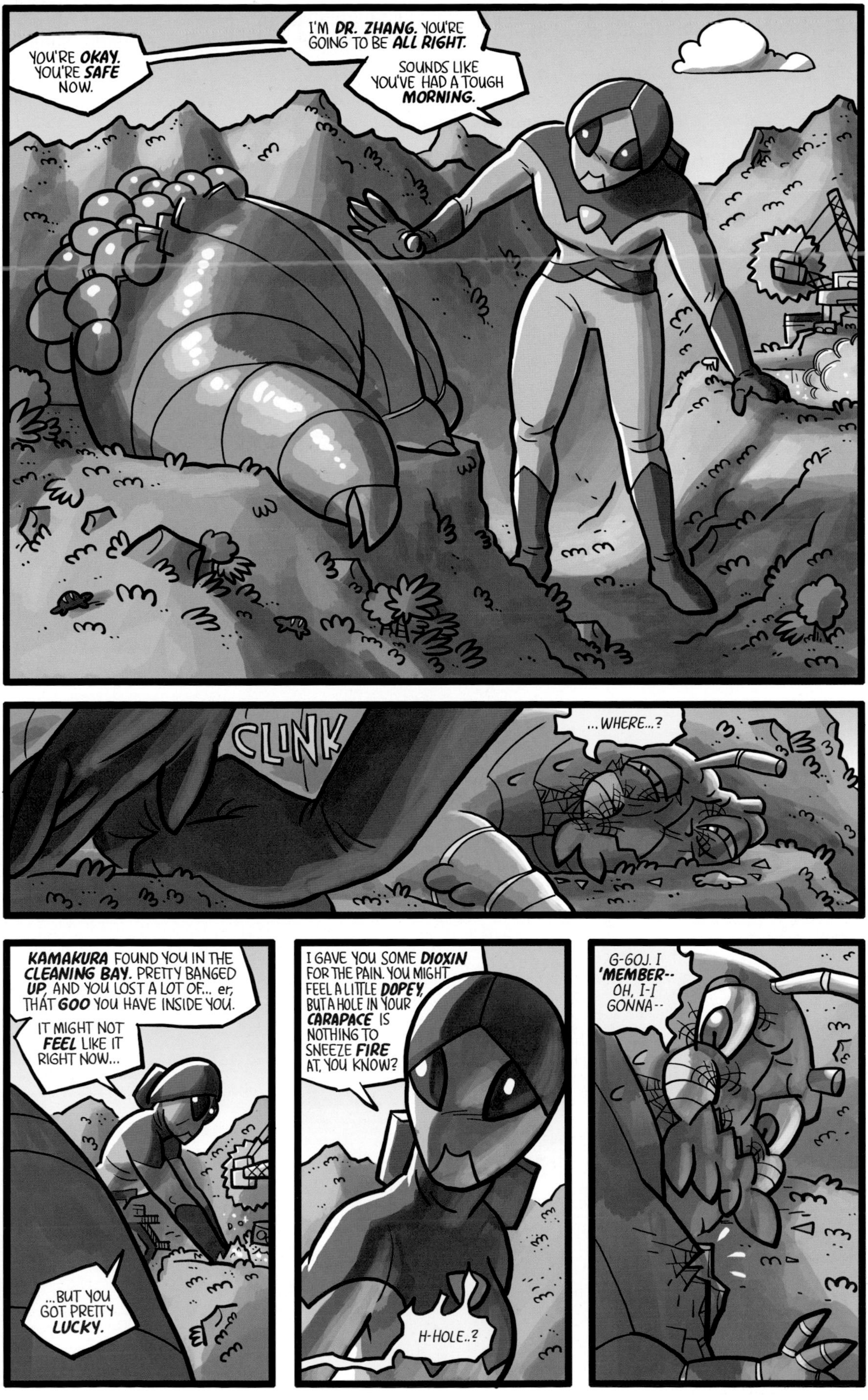

YOU'RE **OKAY.** YOU'RE **SAFE** NOW.

I'M **DR. ZHANG.** YOU'RE GOING TO BE **ALL RIGHT.**

SOUNDS LIKE YOU'VE HAD A TOUGH **MORNING.**

MY **FATHER** PULLED ME OUT OF BED BEFORE **DAWN** AND AS WE RUSHED TO HIGHER **GROUND,** I HEARD IT ROARING BEHIND US.

THE **CREATURE** HAD BEEN AWAKENED BY A MELTING POLAR **ICE CAP,** AND WAS **IRON-** AND **ELECTRICITY-DEFICIENT.**

I COULD TELL HE DIDN'T **WANT** TO BE HERE.

I COULD TELL HE DIDN'T **ASK** TO BE SPAWNED.

BUT HE HAD NO **OPTIONS.** HE HAD NO OTHER **RESOURCES.**

I KNEW THAT WE AS A SOCIETY WERE THE ONES WHO HAD MADE HIM INTO AN OUTCAST.
WE WERE THE ONES WHO HAD MADE THEM ALL INTO MONSTERS.

AND I KNEW I HAD TO SAVE THEM.

I WAS THE FIRST OF MY FAMILY TO GO TO UNIVERSITY, AND THEN TO VETERINARIAN SCHOOL.
AND I KNEW THAT PRISON-- KAIJUMAX -- WAS THE PLACE I COULD DO THE MOST GOOD.

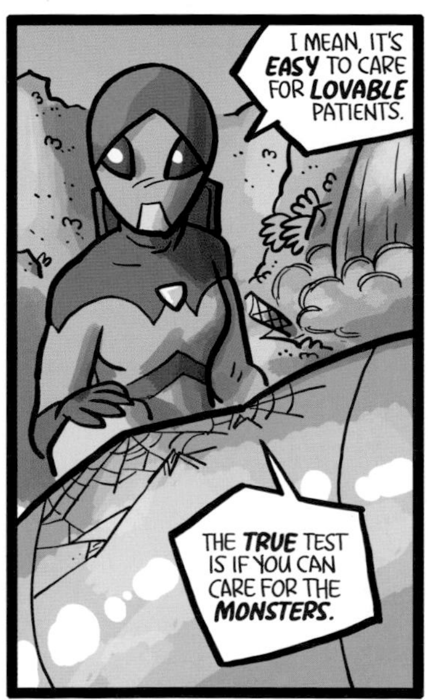
I MEAN, IT'S EASY TO CARE FOR LOVABLE PATIENTS.
THE TRUE TEST IS IF YOU CAN CARE FOR THE MONSTERS.

T-TERRIBLE THING... HAPPENED ME...
I KNOW. IT'S OKAY.

I'M HERE TO TAKE CARE OF YOU.

CHECK-IN

CHECK-IN
JEONG
JIN-WOOK

YO, LIZZA, YOU **HEARD**? THEY GOT THE **GLOW** BACK ON THE POUND NOW. AND IT'S THE **GOOD** STUFF, TOO-- THEY AIN'T **CUTTIN'** IT WITH THE **238** THE WAY THEY **USETA**.
I **HEARD**.
AND I HEARD YOU A STRAIGHT-UP **ANGLE** FOR IT, TOO, LIZZA. CRAWLIN' AROUND ON ALL FOURS, **BEGGIN'** FOR A TASTE.

WHAT? MEGAFAUNA, I'LL **STOMP** YOUR ASS--
CHILL, LIZZA, YOU KNOW I'M JUST **ROASTING** YOU.
?

DAMN it.
JEONG here.
Got an **ALTERCATION** at station **TSU-FOUR**. Handling it **NOW**.

OKAY, ALL RIGHT. THAT'S ENOUGH.
YOU SHOBIJIN CAN GO SING YOUR LITTLE SONGS SOMEWHERE ELSE, GET ME?
YO, WHOA, WHOA! WHAT'S WITH THE ARMOR, MAN?
WE JUST REDKING AROUND, NO NEED TO GO ALL FIVE LIONS ON US.

ARMOR? WHAT ARE YOU...? SHUT IT, CLOAKER. MOVE ALONG TO YOUR CRATERS.
YOU KEEP TALKIN' RADIATION LIKE THAT, IT'S GONNA GET REAL AROUND HERE, REAL FAST.

YOU EVOLVE WITHOUT EARS? MOVE!
I HEARD, I HEARD! WE'RE GOIN', YA HACK.

NO BACKROAR, OR I'LL--
?

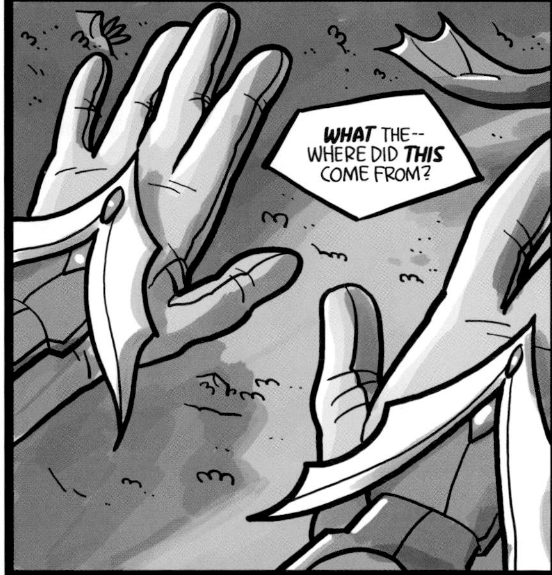
WHAT THE-- WHERE DID THIS COME FROM?

ERRNT
ATTENTION, ALL POINTS -- MEDICAL EMERGENCY IN UCHU BLOCK.

ERRNTERRNTERRNT
REPEAT: ALL AVAILABLE GUARDS TO UCHU BLOCK.
KEIKO -- THIS IS JEONG. RESPONDING NOW.
GUPTA!
C'MON, MAN, WE GOTTA GO!

Yeah, yeah.
I HEARD ya.
As if I don't got ENOUGH problems.

ZOM
HEY, WHAT'RE YOU ALL TOOLED UP FOR? IT'S JUST GONNA BE SOME ELECTRO-TWEAKER JUMPIN' OFF, TRYIN' TO GET IN THE INFIRMARY.
WHAT THOSE CLOAKERS WON'T DO TO GET SOME OF THAT DIOXY.

I MEAN, HELL, IT'S WHAT THEY'RE GONNA DO TO THEMSELVES, SO LET 'EM, YOU KNOW?
LET 'EM O.D., IF THEY'RE SO KEEN ON IT, IS WHAT I SAY.

WHAT'S ONE LIZZA LESS IN THIS LOUSY DUM--?

OH, NO.

DON'T **PUSH** ME, MAN-- I DIDN'T DO **NOTHIN'**.
SHUT UP AND **MOVE** IT, YA **MACCENME.**
LORD, WHAT A **MESS.**
GET THE **EVIDENCE.** BAG THIS **UP.**

AAH, THAT'S **URANIUM.** I DIDN'T EVEN KNOW THAT WAS BACK ON THE **POUND.**
IDIOT
NO **WONDER** HE **O.D.**ed. JUNKIE'S PROBABLY USED TO THE **DEPLETED** STUFF--
KEEP IT **MOVIN'**--

GET THE **QUAD-BELAZ.** LET'S CART HIM OVER TO THE **MORGUE.**
HE'S GOING **OUT.** ZHANG CAN GO AND DO **TIME OF DEATH** LATER.
GUPTA? YOU **IN** THERE?

NO! HELL NO! HE'S **ALIVE!** YOU GET DR. ZHANG **NOW** AND YOU **SAVE** THIS PRISONER!
YOU HEAR ME?? YOU GO TO THE **INFIRMARY** AND **TELL** ZHANG--

"SHE NEEDS TO DROP WHATEVER CRAP SHE'S DOING AND GET HERE NOW!"
GOT YOU ALL CLEANED UP. OKAY, GOOD. YOUR WOUND IS ALREADY STARTING TO HEAL.
LET ME GUESS. YOU WERE CREATED WHEN A BOMBER WITH A NUCLEAR PAYLOAD CRASHED?

NNGH. YES-- A-ALEUTIAN ISLANDS. S-SEVENTY-TWO. NN--
I SEE A LOT OF THAT. YOUR TYPE HEALS FAST.
A LOT OF PEOPLE TAKE IT TO MEAN YOU DON'T FEEL PAIN, BUT THAT'S NOT TRUE, IS IT?
HNNGH. NO-- HHURTS.
SHRI

P-PRESSURE. NNGH--
OKAY. LET'S TAKE A QUICK LOOK AT THE INSIDE. THERE MIGHT BE A SPLINTER LEFT FROM WHOMEVER ATTACKED YOU.

THE TISSUE UNDERNEATH DOES SEEM A LITTLE DISPLACED. MAYBE I CAN GO IN BEFORE YOUR WOUND COMPLETELY--
eh?
DR. ZHANG!!

WE NEED YOU AT UCHU BLOCK RIGHT AWAY--
WE'VE GOT AN OVERDOSE AND HE'S FLATLINING.
WHAT?! AND YOU'RE JUST GETTING ME NOW??
I JUST NEED TO GET MY CRASH-RIG AND I'LL BE RIGHT THERE.

WHAT ABOUT THIS PATIENT, DOCTOR?
HE'S OKAY-- HE'S STABLE. YOU CAN GET HIM BACK TO HIS CRATER, MARIKO.
HHNNGH..

YOU'LL BE FINE. YOU'RE HEALING AND THERE'S NO INFECTION.
KAMAKURA WILL TAKE YOU BACK.
DOCTOR, QUICKLY!
BUT-- HHNNGH- F-FEEL TERRIBLE--

HUHH
"I D-DON'T THINK I'M OKAY..."
ARE-- ARE YOU DOING IT RIGHT?

HUHH
I MEAN, IS HIS HEART EVEN ON THAT SIDE OF HIS CHEST??
GUPTA, I'M DOING EVERY-THING I CAN!

HUHH
COME ON, LIVE, YOU SPAWN OF A BITCH--
BACK OFF, WILL YOU?!

GET OUT OF HERE, GUPTA! SINCE WHEN DO YOU CARE IF ANYONE LIVES OR DIES?
YOU HAVE TO SAVE HIM, DO YOU HEAR ME?

I'M TRYING AS HARD AS I CAN, GOJ DAMN IT!
DON'T YOU SEE THAT??

I'M TRYING TO SAVE HIM AS HARD AS I CAN...
"WHAT'S HAPPENING IN THERE, MAN? SOMEONE SICK?

NONE OF YOUR **BEESWAX**, INMATE. WE'RE IN **LOCKDOWN**. GET TO YOUR **CRATERS** OR I'LL **SPARKLER-KICK** YOU INTO NEXT **WEEK**.
WE'RE GOIN', WE'RE GOIN'.

YOU **TOO**, PEEPIN' **BILLY**. THIS AIN'T YOUR **CONCERN**.
snrff
B-BUT OVER **THERE**, THAT'S--

LISTEN, THAT'S NOT EVEN WHAT THIS IS **ABOUT**. THIS IS A BUSY **DAY**, ALRIGHT? SO **GET**--
snff
URGHH...
BUT **WAIT! WAIT!!**

ELECTROGOR!!

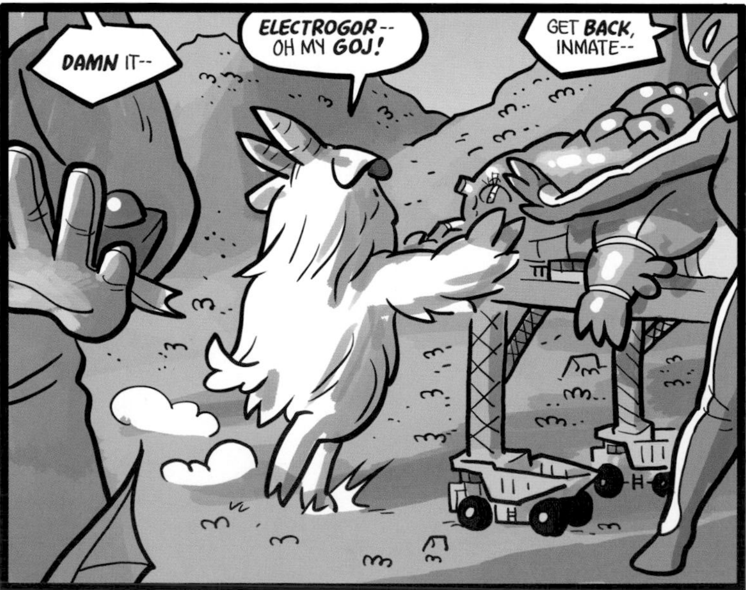
DAMN IT--
ELECTROGOR-- OH MY **GOJ**!
GET **BACK**, INMATE--

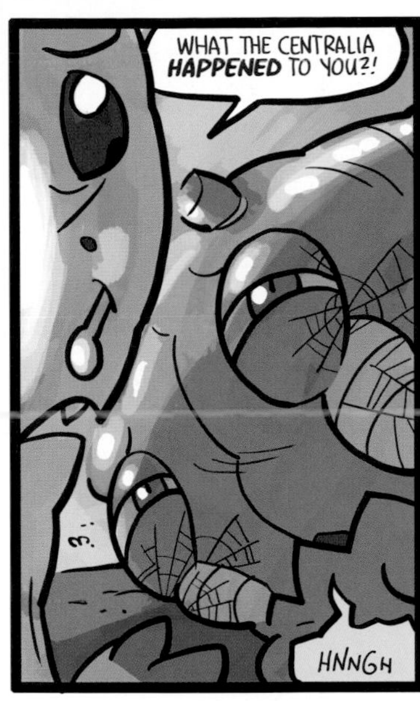
WHAT THE CENTRALIA **HAPPENED** TO YOU?!
HNNGH

COME ON, INMATE, **MOVE** IT.
:nnf: WHO **DID** THIS?
WHO-- :nnf:
WHO **DID** THIS TO YOU?

:hnff: LET ME **GO!** I'LL **FIX** THIS FOR YOU, **ELECTROGOR!**

I'LL **KILL** HIM FOR YOU. I'LL REDKING **KILL** HIM!

SHUT UP, YOU ZOOKY-ASS **CRYP.** YOU AIN'T KILLIN' **ANYONE.**
YOU THINK A NOSE FULL OF **SULPHUR** MAKES YOU A **WARRIOR. GET** BACK IN YOUR DAMN **CRATER** AND SLEEP IT **OFF.**
HNG-- **OOF!**
GET YOUR GOJ-DAMN HANDS **OFF** ME, YOU REDKING **MOBILE SUIT!**

WHAT?
WHAT'S THAT YOU **BLEAT** AT ME, INMATE?
uh...

THAP
W-WAIT!
WAIT!!

KRAK

HhkkgGg
YOU...

Y-YOU SHOULD HAVE **LISTENED.**
ZZT

SH-SHOULD HAVE **LISTENED.**
BEE BO BEE BO BEE BO BEE BO BEE BO BEE BO BEE BO BEE BO

BOBEEBOB

I COULDN'T--

I COULDN'T **SAVE** HIM. I-I TRIED **EVERYTHING.** I-I JUST **COULDN'T.**

sniff

HEY.

GIRL, HOW **YOU** DOIN'? LOOKS LIKE YOU ALL **ALONE** OVER HERE.
AND LOOKIN' **SO SAD.**

YOU'RE NOT-- Y-YOU **INMATES** ARE SUPPOSED TO BE IN YOUR **CRATERS** RIGHT NOW.
IT'S A **LOCKDOWN**. IT'S--IT'S FOR YOUR OWN **SAFETY**.

RIGHT. YEAH, I **HEARD**. BUT HERE I **AM**.
WHERE I **AIN'T** SUPPOSED TO **BE**. ALL **ALONE** WITH YOU IN HERE. YOU **SCARED?**

NO...

I'M NOT SCARED AT **ALL**.

HNNGGh

episode 5

怪獣マックス

We're **BACK** with **KENJI** and the **CHOOKYBEAR** on the **MORNING KREATURE KREW** here on **108.7**, the **BATTLE-ANTHEM!**

We're got an uninterrupted block of **TUNES** coming at you in just a **MINUTE**, but...

CHOOKY CHA-CHOOKY!

HA HA! That's **RIGHT**, Chooky-bear, the **TRAFFIC REPORT!**

Looks like we've got some **SLOWDOWN** in the air over the **MARSHALLS**, and some **RUBBERNECKERS** are holding things up after a minor **AIRFOIL-BENDER** near **TONGA.**

CHOOKY!

You **KNOW** it, Chooky-Bear! This **STORM** isn't helping anything **EITHER!**

Oh, for God's SAKE.
DAMN it.
EVOLVE MY HEAR--
click
Oh, come ON!
What is-- HEY! Hey YOU!!

PULL over. That ISLAND, right THERE.

Son of a--
It WOULD have to happen in THIS %$&?!ing weather, WOULDN'T it.
What the HELL, man? How about sharing the SKIES, huh?

LISTEN, pal...
Oh, HEY. WAIT. You're with Team H.E.R.O.I.S.M.! OKAY. Listen, man, I'm on the job TOO.
Lieutenant NGUYEN. Team G.R.E.A.T. Okay, we can work this OUT.

Okay. WHATEVER. GOOD. Let me give you my INFORMATION.
JEEZ, man, if you guys would look outside your CAGES a little bit and start SEEING hovercycles, we'd ALL live a little LONGER.
YEAH. I %$&?!ing HEARD you the FIRST time.

Whoa, WHOA. Listen. I'm just SAYING.
LOOK at your SPACE BATTLESHIP here, man. There's barely a scratch ON it.
My HOG'S all but TOTALED.
Screw YOU, Nguyen. If you would stop riding like a WON-WON-WON-WONDER MORON, this wouldn't HAPPEN.

LISTEN, guy, THAT'S a little out of LINE, don't you--
HNPH!!
HEY! What's the DEAL, man?!
SHUT IT!
If you would get out of my %$&?!ing WAY I could get to %$&?!ing WORK.

You want to INSULT me? You want to TEST me?
You want to %$&?!ing SEE who's the bigger MAN??
"Looks like we've got a STORM brewing, eh, sir?"

Hmm? Oh, yes, it looks like it may hit by TONIGHT.
Nature's FURY. The REAL stuff, this time.

Anyway, YOU'RE early, Dr. Zhang.
Er, YESSIR. I uh, I wanted to get a JUMP on things.

ELECTROGOR has a THERAPY appointment after that INCIDENT in the WATERFALLS a few days ago.
pff: Oh. RIGHT. HIM. THERAPY, huh?
Well, get him to tell you who DID it if you CAN. We can't have that HAPPENING.
Otherwise, I don't know what he needs THERAPY for. He should just DEAL with his problems and get ON with it, like HUMANS.

Oh, sir, I don't KNOW. TRAUMA has psycho-logical FACTORS that we can't just--
BRINNG
EXCUSE me, just a MOMENT.
Hello. Warden KANG here.
Yes, there's a JEONG who works here.
WAIT-- you say he's WHAT??!

Look OUT, he's-- SKRRK

FLANK him, FLANK HIM!

HQ, this is NGUYEN! We've got a TJ-28 here, in PROGRESS!

the MEGA-MONSTER BATTLE at HOME

HA HA! YOU GOT ME! YOU FOUND ME, LI'L BOY! THAT WAS A GOOD JOB!
THAT WAS PRETTY EASY. YOU'RE KINDA BIG, YOU KNOW.
YEAH! I AM! THIS IS SO FUN, LI'L BOY! I'M SO LUCKY YOU ARE MY BEST FRIEND!

I GUESS...
BUT I DON'T KNOW HOW GOOD OF FRIENDS WE ARE IF YOU WON'T EVEN DO MY LITTLE JOKE.
BUT--

BUT LI'L BOY, THAT WOULD HURT MY DAD. TH-THOSE LEAVES--YOU SAY THEY MAKE HIM SICK.
M-MY DAD A GOOD GUY-- HE USE TO BE A FORCE OF NATURE, BUT NOW HE JUST A PROTECTOR. NOW HE SAY HE NEVER HURT ANY--
WHOOFY!!

YOU WORTHLESS PIECE OF AMBERGRIS, GET OVER HERE! WE ARE SETTING UP FOR THE BIG MEETING TODAY.
IF YOU WEREN'T PLAYING LIKE A FOOL, YOU'D KNOW THIS.

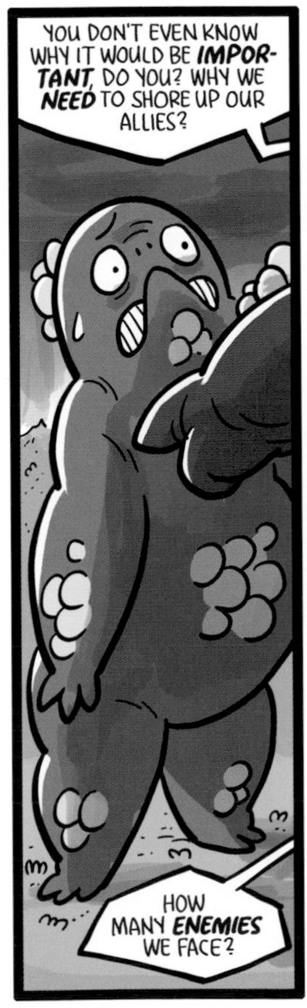
YOU DON'T EVEN KNOW WHY IT WOULD BE IMPORTANT, DO YOU? WHY WE NEED TO SHORE UP OUR ALLIES?
HOW MANY ENEMIES WE FACE?

pfah
YOU WOULD LET THE MAKETO GANG JUST ROLL OVER US.
LET THEM HOLD UP THE BALL, AND SHOUT "RETURN!" AND THAT WOULD BE THE END.
YOU WOULD, WOULDN'T YOU?

NO, DAD, I--I NEVER--
LI'L BOY, I SORRY. I GOT TO GO. IT'S IMPORTAN--
?
LI'L BOY? WHERE YOU GO AGAIN?
I-I COME BACK TO PLAY LATER, LI'L BOY! I--
WHOOFY!

バカ!
GET OVER HERE NOW, OR YOU'LL FEEL THE BACK OF MY FLIPPER!
"NOW, I WANT YOU TO KNOW THAT THIS IS A SAFE SPACE."

SAFE TO TALK. SAFE TO EXPRESS YOURSELF. THERE IS NO JUDGMENT HERE.
IT'S VERY IMPORTANT TO ME THAT YOU'RE COMFORTABLE, AND THAT YOU FEEL LISTENED TO, hmm?
ELECTROGOR, I'VE BEEN TOLD YOU HAVEN'T LEFT YOUR CRATER FOR SEVERAL DAYS. ARE YOU DOING ALL RIGHT?
HNNGH... I-I'M FINE. J-JUST CAUGHT A... DECOMPOSITION MICROBE O-OR SOMETHING...
DON'T NEED TO BE HERE... JUST NEED TO R-REST A LITTLE.
Ah, NOW, ELECTROGOR, I FELT LIKE YOU AND I HAD AN UNDERSTANDING.
HONESTY IS CRUCIAL IN A SITUATION LIKE THIS.
EVEN IF IT MAKES US FEEL VULNERABLE.

IN FACT--
SHING!
NNGH..?

ZOOF
I want you to SEE. I'M vulnerable TOO. And I'm here to HELP you. That is my ONLY GOAL.
HGN... Y-YES, but I, uh, I UNDERSTAND your WORDS better when you... NOT-PUNY.
I-I just not want to... uh, ROAR about it.
Very WELL. I HEAR what you're SAYING.
I really DO. The SHAME, the feeling of HELPLESSNESS.

ZOM
BEING ATTACKED IN THIS MANNER CAN BE ESPECIALLY DIFFICULT FOR CREATURES LIKE YOU.
YOU ARE USED TO BEING STRONG. POWERFUL. THE PROTECTOR. THE KING.
BUT SOMEONE HAS TAKEN THAT FROM YOU, HAVEN'T THEY?

YOU ALWAYS THOUGHT YOUR EXOSKELETON COULD KEEP YOU FROM HARM. BUT SOMEONE PUT A HOLE IN IT. ISN'T THAT RIGHT?
ELECTROGOR...
...CAN YOU TALK ABOUT IT?

IT MADE ME FEEL...
THE WORLD GREW UP AROUND ME. EVERYTHING. ALL AROUND MY EYES.
I--I FELT LIKE I WAS TINY.

HELPLESS. LIKE ANYTHING COULD SQUISH ME. ANYTHING AT ALL.
I-I FELT...

I FELT LIKE ONE OF YOU.

I SEE. AND THE MON WHO DID THIS...
SOMEONE WHO WOULD TAKE ALL THAT AWAY FROM YOU... WHY WOULD HE DO THAT?
I DON'T...
I-I DON'T KNOW WHY.

"EXACTLY. THERE IS NO REASON WHY SOMEONE SHOULD EVER DO THIS TO ANOTHER BEING.
"IF YOU'LL PARDON THE EXPRESSION, IT'S MONSTROUS.
"THIS SHOULDN'T EVER HAPPEN TO ANYONE. WE CAN'T ALLOW THIS TO HAPPEN AGAIN, ELECTROGOR."

YOU WILL BE PROTECTED. YOU CAN TALK HERE, IN THIS SAFE SPACE. THIS MONSTER EXCLUSION ZONE.
WE CAN SIMPLY KEEP AN EYE OUT FOR THIS INMATE, MAKE SURE HE DOESN'T DO THIS TO ANYONE ELSE.
I--
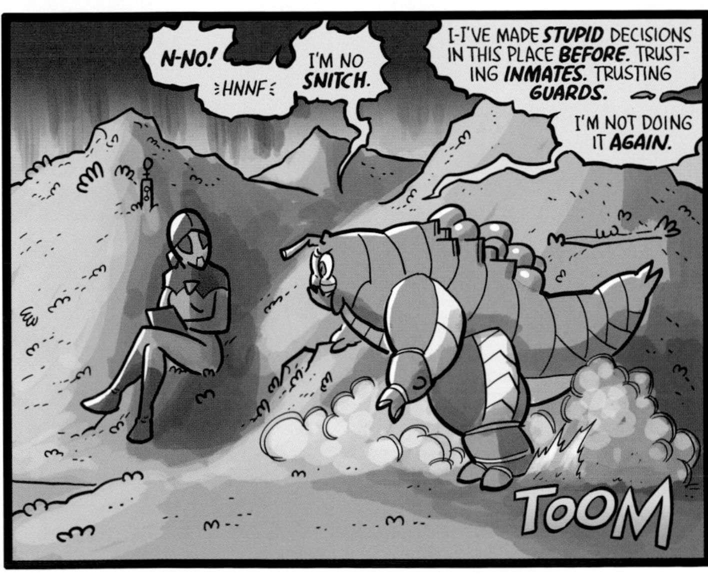
N-NO!
HNNF
I'M NO SNITCH.
I-I'VE MADE STUPID DECISIONS IN THIS PLACE BEFORE. TRUSTING INMATES. TRUSTING GUARDS.
I'M NOT DOING IT AGAIN.
TOOM

YOU'RE FREE TO LEAVE, OF COURSE. I'LL HAVE KAMAKURA TAKE YOU BACK.
BUT LOOK AT YOURSELF.

"LOOK AT WHAT HE'S REDUCED YOU TO."
All RIGHT, here we are. Back at your CRATER.
You DOING okay?

I mean, when I found you at the WATER-FALLS the other day, ATTACKED like that, I didn't know if you were going to pull THROUGH.
I'm glad you DID.
So, uh, ANYWAY.

"That stuff with your KIDS, too, that you TOLD me about.
"Did you figure something OUT?"

Uh, yes, I uh... I OKAY.
And I... I guess I figure something out for CHILDS.
THANK you.
Thank you for THINKING on me.

Hey, don't WORRY about it. I was CURIOUS.
Y'know, I'm here to HELP.
OKAY. Have a good DAY.
WAIT.

The Dr. ZHANG, she ask me a QUESTION.
I not TELL her, but now I uh...
I AGAIN-THINK.
ZONNG
Please...

"... can you DELIVER to her a MESSAGE?"
JEONG.

HEY, kid.

Sounds like you've had a pretty hard **DAY**.

NORMALLY at this point, your man would be WRIST-IMMOBILIZED, ELECTRO-STASISED, and halfway to HONG KONG.
You'll notice he's NOT.
I DO see that, Colonel. I appreciate your CALL, and I appreciate your DISCRETION in this matter.
I don't know why I shouldn't do it NOW, though, Warden.
Even with no loss of LIFE, this has been an EXPENSIVE DAY for TEAM G.R.E.A.T..

"Can we make a DEAL?"
LI'L BOY?

LI'L BOY? I-I'M BACK. I JUST HAD TO TALK TO MY DAD 'BOUT STUFF.
HEY LI'L--

HEY, WHAT IS THIS?
I WOULDN'T TOUCH THAT IF I WERE YOU.

LI'L BOY! WHAT IS THIS? WHAT ARE YOU MAKING?
EXCUSE ME, WHOOFY. MOVE OUT OF THE WAY, PLEASE. I HAVE TO PUT MORE WOOD ON MY FIRE.

UH, OKAY.
BUT WHAT IS THIS? WHAT ARE YOU COOKING? IT LOOK LIKE SOUP.
IT'S OKAY. YOU DON'T NEED TO KNOW. YOU DON'T WANT TO HELP ME ANYWAY.

BUT I DO WANT TO HELP YOU, LI'L BOY. WHAT DO YOU NEED HELP WITH?
YOUR DAD IS MEAN TO YOU. HE MAKES YOU FEEL BAD ALL THE TIME. I DON'T THINK THAT'S RIGHT.
I'M A PERSON WHO LIKES YOU AND THINKS YOU ARE VERY SMART AND VERY GOOD.
BUT YOU DON'T WANT TO HELP ME. YOU WOULD RATHER MAKE YOUR DAD HAPPY THAN ME.

BUT...
ALL I WANT TO DO IS PLAY A SIMPLE JOKE. A JOKE THAT WOULD HELP YOU.
BUT YOU WON'T EVEN DO IT WITH ME.
SO I GUESS I DON'T EVEN CARE WHAT YOU THINK ANYMORE.

B-BUT...
O-OKAY.
I DO IT.

REALLY?
YEAH, I HELP YOU. I KNOW YOU A GOOD FRIEND, AND I-I KNOW IT WILL BE FUNNY, L-LIKE YOU SAY.

OH, WHOOFY! THAT'S WONDERFUL! YOU ARE SO GOOD! SO SMART!
THIS IS GOING TO BE SO FUNNY!
SUCH A FUNNY JOKE FOR EVERYONE!

Y-YEAH. M-MAYBE EVEN MY DAD THINK IT'S FUNNY.
OH, WHOOFY!

WHOOFY, I LOVE YOU.

I-I LOVE YOU, TOO, LI'L BOY.
HA HA. THIS GOING BE SO FUNNY.
MY DAD'S MEETING ABOUT TO START. SHOULD WE TAKE IT DOWN THERE NOW?
TAKE WHAT?

UH, THAT. THE SOUP YOU MAKE WITH THE LEAVES.
YOU KNOW, F-FOR A JOKE.
OH, THAT.
THAT IS A GREAT IDEA. GOOD THINKING.

BUT I DIDN'T MAKE THAT, WHOOFY. I COULDN'T.
YOU MUST'VE.
ONLY YOU ARE SMART ENOUGH TO DO THIS.
YOU'VE ALWAYS BEEN THE SMART ONE, ALL ALONG.

"DOESN'T THAT MAKE YOU HAPPY?"
OMG
WAHH

OH NO! I'M IN PRISON!!
OMG
WAHH
B
U
T
GWAIYAA! WHAT A HOTTIE!
I'M ACEY DEUCY!
HOW CAN I GET HIS ATTENTION?
STAY CALM, I GOT THIS
E-EXCUSE ME... UH...?
TONGUE TIED!
I LOVE YOUU
STOP IT WHAT ARE YOU DOING
OW
PAK
YES SENPAI
WHAT IN THE--
WHAT IS THIS? WHERE DID THIS COME FROM?
I WOULD THINK YOU WOULD KNOW.
OBVIOUSLY IT'S A JOURNAL, TELLING ME A DIFFERENT SIDE THAN WHAT YOU SAID BEFORE.
NOW, THERAPY REQUIRES TRUST, AS I SAID.
I REALLY EXPECTED BETTER OF YOU THAN TO LIE ABOUT BEING ATTACKED.
LIE?!

I-I'M **NOT** LYING. I-I TOLD YOU, ZONN **ATTACKED** ME IN THE **WATERFALL**. HE-HE STUCK SOMETHING IN MY **SIDE**.
YOU SAW THE WOUND **YOURSELF**. YOU **TREATED** IT. YOU **SAID** THERE MIGHT BE SOMETHING LEFT **IN** THERE.

I **DO** AGREE THAT YOU WERE **HURT**, BUT IT DOESN'T LOOK LIKE IT HAPPENED THE WAY YOU **SAY**, ELECTROGOR.
IT SOUNDS LIKE YOU WENT **LOOKING** FOR TROUBLE, AND YOU **FOUND** IT.

HE GAVE YOU THIS **"JOURNAL"**, DIDN'T HE? HE **FED** YOU THAT WHOLE STORY. HE'S **MANIPULATING** YOU AND YOU DON'T EVEN **SEE** IT.
YOU LIE!!

ALL YOU 'NILLA **CRYBABIES** ARE ALL THE **SAME**. YOU WANT TO TEMPT **GOOD** MONSTERS -- **ANTI-HEROES** -- AND THEN **LIE** AND **BLACKMAIL** THEM FOR YOUR OWN **AMUSEMENT**.
HE **TOLD** ME. YOUR TYPE **ALWAYS** TRIES TO **DO** THIS TO HIM, BUT I'M NOT GOING TO LET YOU SO-CALLED **"BATTLE JUSTICE WARRIORS"** WIN THIS TIME.
NNF-- BUT--
HE'S **LYING** TO YOU! YOU-YOU **SAW** IT! YOU **S-SAW** WHAT HE **DID** TO ME! I'M **STILL** IN PAIN!!

OH, YOU THINK YOU STILL HAVE SOMETHING **WRONG** FROM THAT ITTY-BITTY **LOVE TAP**, YOU LITTLE **FRIENDLY RARE-BEAST?**
MAYBE WE **DO** NEED A LITTLE **SURGERY**, HUH?
WHAT? N-NO! LET **GO!**

LET'S OPEN YOU **UP** AND SEE WHAT'S **IN** THERE IF YOU'RE GOING TO BE SUCH A **LARVA** ABOUT IT.
WHAT ARE YOU-- **STOP!**
STOP!!

YOU NEVER **THINK** ABOUT THE MONS YOU'RE **HURTING** WHEN YOU DO THIS, **DO** YOU?
WELL, **NOW** YOU **WILL**.
STOP!!

STOP

OWW!
GUARD! KAMAKURA!!

I'M HERE! WHAT--
HE--
HE'S GONE CRAZY-- HE ATTACKED ME!
NGH-- NO, I--

ALL RIGHT, GET UP, INMATE. YOU NEVER TOUCH A GUARD OR A DOCTOR. YOU'RE GOING TO THE HOLE FOR THIS.
NGH. NO, PLEASE--

I CAN'T BELIEVE THIS. COME ON. ON YOUR FEET.
PLEASE... NO, THAT'S NOT-- PLEASE...

PLEA--

WINK

MY LOYAL **ALLIES**, WE HAVE FACED MANY DARK **TIMES** OVER OUR LIVES.
PITTED **AGAINST** EACH OTHER, IMPRISONED **UNDERGROUND**, **POISONED**, **DETONATED**, **FED RADIATION**, AND FORCED TO FIGHT **UNDIGNIFIED ENEMIES** FOR HUMAN **MASTERS**.
BUT THROUGH IT **ALL**, WE HAVE **SHOWN** THAT WHEN WE **TEAM UP** -- WHEN WE **ALL-OUT ATTACK** -- THAT WE **CANNOT** BE CONTROLLED.
WE ARE **HUBRIS**. WE ARE **UNCHECKED MILITARISM**. WE ARE **TRULY** THE **FULL FURY** OF **NATURE**.
CLAP CLAP CLAP

CLAP CLAP
HEAR, HEAR!
AND YET THE COMING GENERATION REFUSES TO TAKE US SERIOUSLY.
WE ARE THOUGHT OF AS OLD-FASHIONED. WEAK, FAT, AND FOOLISH. OBJECTS OF RIDICULE.
PSST!!

HEY!
STOP FIDGETING! YOU'RE GOING TO SPILL THE POT!
START LOOKING FOR AN OPENING. WHEN HE'S LOOKING AWAY FROM HIS FOOD.
OUR ANSWER TO SUCH A
INSULT MUST BE SWIFT,

L-LI'L BOY, I DON'T KNOW ABOUT THIS. IT SEEM LIKE IT NOT GOING TO WORK.
SHUT UP! IT'S GOING TO BE SO FUNNY, WHOOFY! HE'LL BE LIKE, "ACK, ACK!"
HE'LL COUGH AND GET ALL SLEEPY.
WHOOFY
HE'LL PROBABLY EVEN HAVE TO GO TO THE BATHROOM ALL OVER THE PLACE, LIKE THAT ONE TIME AGAINST THE ARMY!

WAIT, H-HOW YOU KNOW ABOUT--
WHOOFY, WHAT DO YOU THINK ABOUT YOUR DAD'S PLAN? I KNOW YOU DON'T LIKE TO FIGHT.
UH...

Y-YEAH, THAT **RIGHT**. I NOT **LIKE** TO FIGHT.
DAD MAKE ME **FIGHT** SOMETIMES. STAND ON MY **TOE** TO MAKE ME **ROAR**. IT **HURT**.
HA! GOOD OLD **WHOOFY! HA HA HA!**
IDIOCY.

THE OPINIONS OF THIS GOJ-DAMN **INCOMPETENT** AREN'T WORTH **LISTENING** TO. LET'S MOVE **ON**, SHALL WE?
IF WE ARE TO **COMBAT** THE INCREASING **INFLUENCE** OF THE **MAKETOGANG** AS WE

ALLIES FROM OTHER **REAS**. I HAVE **INVITED** ONE OF THEM TO BE
HEY!
HEY! DO IT **NOW!** THEY'RE GOING TO BE **EATING** IN JUST A **SECOND!**
BUT--

AH, **HERE** HE IS.

NOW! NOW! HE'S **DISTRACTED!** DO IT **NOW!!**
ZONN! JOIN US! I'M SO

TATION PRECEDES YOU HERE IN KAIJUMAX.
YOUR WORK FOR OU NUMEROUS **ALLIES NAGOYA** AND THE

ABLE TO **EVADE** OLD 'HIROSHI LAW' FOR EXTENDED PERIODS

YOU **DID** IT!
YOU'RE SO **GREAT!**
YOU'RE **INCREDIBLE!!**

WHOOFY, YOU'RE THE **VERY BEST FRIEND** I EVER **HAD**.

A TOAST!! TO ALLIES, BOTH SHOWA AND MILLENNIUM.
TO MEGA-MONSTER DOMINATION NOW AND IN THE FUTURE.
...AND TO OUR ENEMIES' BANISHMENT TO THE BOTTOM OF THE OCEANS!
乾杯！

EAT, EAT, EVERYONE, PLEASE. WE HAVE, ahem, PROCURED PLENTY JUST FOR THIS EVENT.
THERE IS MORE THAN ENOUGH FOR EVERYONE.

CHUP

DELICIOUS. MY MON KORUGON HAS OUTDONE HIMSELF.
FRIENDS, I AM BLESSED TO BE SURROUNDED BY SUCH LOYALT--
HKK
EXCUSE ME, I...

HHKK KKHHKK
AAKK KKHHGAAK
B-BOSS?
KUMICHO? WHAT IS IT?

KTOOM
HHKAAK!!

KKGAAH HKK

KKKUHH

NUH.
D-DAD?
BOSS! HEY, BOSS!
ARE YOU OKAY??
OH MY GOJ
HO COULD
DONE THIS
OH MY GOJ
GET SOMEBODY

H MY GOJ
OH MY GOJ
YOU! RUN AN
FIND SOMEO
IT'S THOSE
MOTHRA-REDKIN
GOATSUCKERS

AWAY FROM HIM--
VE HIM NITROGEN
OH GOJ--
BOSS!!
CAN'T BE
HAPPENING...

D-DADDY? DADDY!!
DADDY!!
'T'S OVER. IT'S
) LATE. THERE'S
NOTHING WE
HOW COULD ANYTHING STOP

NO NO NO
N-NO NO NO
DAAAAA
WHOOFY--
HE'S DEAD.
STAND BACK.
WHOOFY!
COME AWAY
FROM HIM!

NO! N-
NAAAWW
D-DADDY,
PLEASE, COME
BACK ALIVE!
ASPLODE A
BOMB AND
COME BACK
ALL RED!
AAAAAHHH
HUH HUH HUH
WHOOFY!
DAMN IT!
WHOOFY! GET
BACK! RIGHT
NOW!

WHOOFY, PLEASE,
COME AWAY FROM HIM.
QUICKLY, NOW.
PLEASE,
SON...

"...THERE'S NO MORE WE
CAN DO FOR HIM."
HEY.
You all
RIGHT?

I'm okay. THANK you,
Warden. I'm SORRY.
Now, no NEED
to be --
N-no, I've got it
TOGETHER now. I, uh,
I'm SORRY you had to go
OUT there just for ME.

LISTEN.
You're the best
we've GOT here.
There's NO ONE
I'd rather GO to in
a PINCH.
So things got a little
DARK EMPEROR out
there for a bit. We ALL
have days like that.
When
we get a little
PROVOKED.
Yeah, I-I
GUESS.
Y-y'know, I always want
to do my BEST, but lately
it's been just so...

... difficult...

JEONG! Come ON! QUICK!
Kid, if you EVER wanted to PROVE yourself, now's the TIME!
SHING

Y-yeah. YEAH.
ZAM
SHING
I-I'm COMING.

ZAM
YOU WITH ME? WE'RE ALMOST THERE. I CAN SEE THE SMOKE JUST OVER--

AAAH

episode

6

怪獣マックス

WHOOFY™

ZZT
ZT
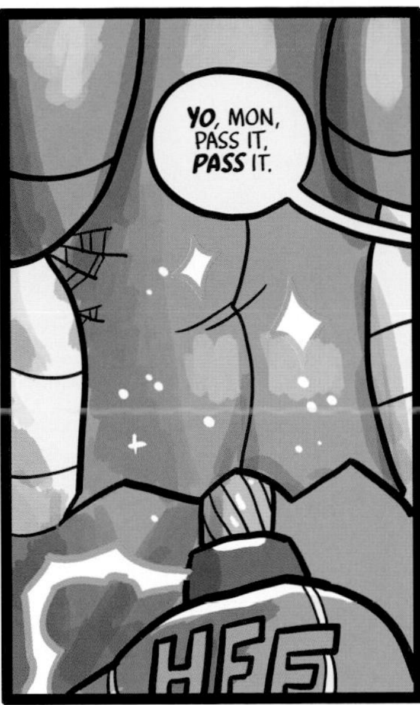
YO, MON, PASS IT, PASS IT.
HFF

GO EASY. THAT STUFF CAN MESS YOU UP.
STRAIGHT UP SCRAMBLE YOUR GANGLIONS AND YOU'LL END UP LIKE MY BUDDY HERE.

YEAH, MEGA-FAUNA! WE ALL STUCK IN HERE, SAME AS YOU!
SEND THAT CRACKLE OVER THIS WAY, 'NILLA, I GOT SOME THINKIN' PARTS I WANT TO FRY, KNOW WHAT I'M SAYIN'?

YOU WAIT YOUR TURN, DING WING.
HFF
LIZZA, I TOLD YOU THAT AIN'T MY NAME.
YOU GOT TO CALL ME GIANT MONSTER TERONGO, TERROR of PAGO PAGO.
THE WHOLE THING.

MON, I DON'T CARE WHAT YOUR MAMA CALL YOU.

YOU ACT LIKE YOU GOT A DING UPSTAIRS, AND YOU THE LOW MON ON THE MITSUME POLE, FOOL, THEN YOU GET A NEW NAME.

WELL, YOU AIN'T GOTTA MAKE ME FEEL INFERIOR ABOUT IT, MEGAFAUNA.

HEY, MON, THIS... LIKE, ELECTRO-STILL YOU GOT, DID YOU RIG THIS ALL YOURSELF?
YOU KNOW IT.
HAD IT READY FOR A WHILE, BUT IT TOOK THAT STORM COMING THROUGH TO CHARGE IT UP.
NONE OF THE BULLS EVEN KNOW THE PYLON'S OFF THE GRID, AND WE GET SOME DANK VOLTS EVERY WEEK OR SO.
HHFFF
snicker

YOU SURPRISED? YO, THERE'S MORE TO ME THAN SPITTIN' FLAME, Y' DIG IT?
I GOT PLANS FOR THIS PLACE, YO.
MOSTLY THEM PLANS INVOLVE GETTIN' TOTALLY DEMOLISHED, BUT YOU KNOW WHAT I MEAN.

YOU WANNA SIT AND LOOK AT IT AWHILE, K-MAX AIN'T SO HARD TO FIGURE OUT.
DON'T TAKE TOO LONG TO SEE ALL THE LITTLE HOLES AND BLIND SPOTS, START SEEING WHAT YOU CAN GET AWAY WITH.
YEAH!
HFFT
WHAT, LIKE ESCAPING?

NAH. I DUNNO. MAYBE YOU COULD, BUT WHAT A HASSLE, YOU KNOW?
THE FUGITIVE LIFE?
AT LEAST HERE I KNOW I GOT THIS SPACE TO SPARK UP WHEN I NEED IT.
HFF
YEAH, BUDDY!!
OUTSIDE WORLD'S TOO SMALL FOR BIG FELLAS LIKE US THESE DAYS.

I MEAN, IF THERE'S A PLAN, THEM PYLONS AIN'T SO HARD TO DISRUPT.
YOU'D NEED A BIG ENERGY SOURCE, I GUESS. AND A RELIABLE SECOND MON.
WOO!!

DING WING'S GOT HIS USES AND ALL, BUT MON, I TELL YOU...
SCREW YOU, CONFORMITY!

BLAT

...HE AIN'T THE **BRIGHTEST.**

INSIDE THESE FORCEFIELDS

ALL RIGHT, INMATE, C'MON, C'MON, C'MON.
I GOT SOME BUYERS, AND I NEED MONEY. HAND OVER THE URANIUM.
YEAH, YEAH.

THAT THE TONE YOU WANT TO TAKE?
HAND OVER THAT GLOW AND MAKE IT QUICK.
NNF
I DON'T HAVE ALL DAY TO FEED YOU COMPLIMENTS.

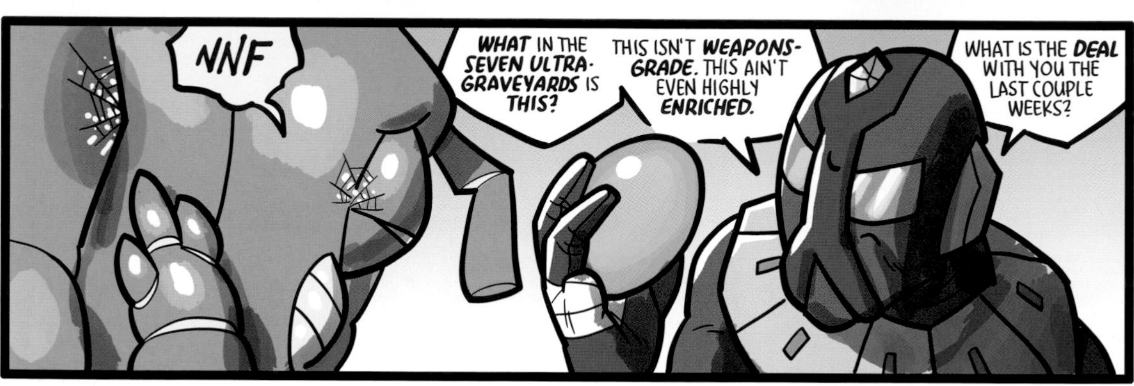
NNF
WHAT IN THE SEVEN ULTRA-GRAVEYARDS IS THIS?
THIS ISN'T WEAPONS-GRADE. THIS AIN'T EVEN HIGHLY ENRICHED.
WHAT IS THE DEAL WITH YOU THE LAST COUPLE WEEKS?

THIS AMBERGRIS BARELY REGISTERS ON THE GEIGER. YOU KEEP GOIN' THE WAY YOU'RE GOIN', AND WE'RE ONLY GONNA GET 238. THE DEPLETED STUFF, YOU HEARD?
AND THEN LIZZAS AIN'T GETTING HIGH AND I AIN'T MAKING MONEY.
YOU UNDERSTAND WHAT THAT MEANS, LIZZA? I NEED THEM RAI-STONES, YOU %&?!ING HEAR ME?
THIS, AFTER ALL I DID FOR YOU. AFTER EVERYTHING.

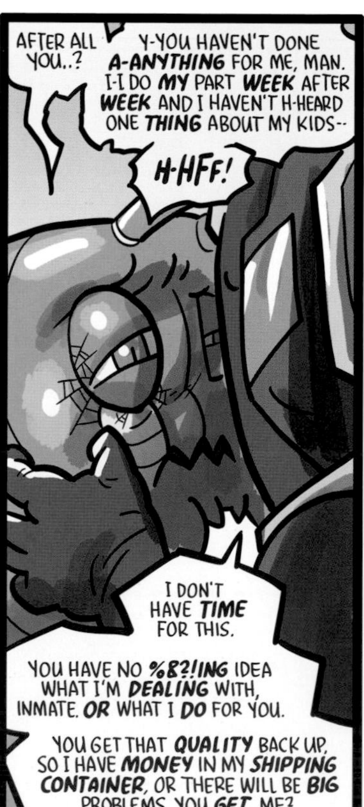
AFTER ALL YOU..?
Y-YOU HAVEN'T DONE A-ANYTHING FOR ME, MAN. I-I DO MY PART WEEK AFTER WEEK AND I HAVEN'T H-HEARD ONE THING ABOUT MY KIDS--
H-HFF!
I DON'T HAVE TIME FOR THIS.
YOU HAVE NO %&?!ING IDEA WHAT I'M DEALING WITH, INMATE. OR WHAT I DO FOR YOU.
YOU GET THAT QUALITY BACK UP, SO I HAVE MONEY IN MY SHIPPING CONTAINER, OR THERE WILL BE BIG PROBLEMS, YOU GET ME?

I DON'T WANT TO HEAR YOU WHINING ABOUT YOUR LARVAE ONE MORE TIME.
MAYBE THEY'RE ALIVE, MAYBE THEY'RE DEAD. IT DON'T MEAN NOTHING TO ME, SO IT DON'T MEAN NOTHING TO YOU.
HNF!
YO, YO! WHAT'S UP, KYODAI?

WHAT'S IT TO YOU? THIS IS A PRIVATE CONVERSATION, FRANKIE.
I AIN'T--
SIGH
LISTEN, AIN'T THIS MON HAD A BAD ENOUGH MONTH, MEGAFAUNA?
GETTIN' JIGER'D IN THE WATERFALLS? SENT TO THE HOLE?

SH-SHUT UP, MON...
I DON'T GIVE A BALLOON-CARRYIN' CRAP ABOUT HIS PROBLEMS.
THAT'S WHY HIS GLOW IS LOW QUALITY? TOO BAD FOR HIM. I GOT TO GET PAID.

AND IF YOU'RE STOMPIN' IN THE WAY OF THAT...
...MAYBE THINGS GET A LITTLE HOT FOR YOU.
MAYBE THAT HAPPENS RIGHT NOW.
STEP ASIDE, INMATE. TIME FOR A LITTLE SEARCH.

YOU JUST NEVER KNOW WHAT YOU'RE GOING TO FIND WHEN YOU TOSS A CRATER.
COME ON, MAN...
DRAGONS LIVE IN THESE THINGS.
SOMETIMES YOU COME ACROSS A LITTLE TREASURE HORDE.

HMM, WHAT'S THIS? LITTLE EXTRA CONTRA-BAND MONEY LYING AROUND FOR ME? THANKS, FRANKEN-STEIN, THAT'S REAL THOUGHTFUL.

OH, BUT THIS? SUCH A MESS. LET ME HELP YOU WITH THAT.
CRASH
LISTEN, MAN...

OR WHAT IF WE GO OVER HERE IN THESE...?
OH OH. OH MY.
FRANKENSTEIN, WHAT IS THIS?
HHH
I DON'T KNOW.
I AIN'T NEVER SEEN THAT BEFORE.
41

AIN'T THAT RIGHT?
UH...

HEY, YEAH, YO, THAT'S ALL ME, KYODAI. Y'KNOW, I MADE THAT. THAT'S ME.
YEAH?

YOU MADE THIS, HUH? USED YOUR BIG MUTANT BRAIN, PUT ALL THIS JUNK TOGETHER, MADE IT WORK?
Y-YEAH, MAN...
TELL IT TO THE MOBILE SUITS, Y'ZOOKY-ASS TWEAKER. YOU COULDN'T PUT TOGETHER A COHERENT SENTENCE.
N-NAW, MAN, THAT'S THE TRUTH. I DID ALL THAT ON MY OWN. S-SOLDERED IT ALL WITH, LIKE, FLAME BREATH, OR SOMETHIN'.

KRAK

YO! BE CAREFUL WITH THAT ONE, KYODAI!!
THAT'S GIANT MONSTER TERONGO, TERROR OF PAGO PAGO YOU GOT THERE!

SHUT UP!
I'M TAKIN' THIS TO IMPOUND, AND THIS CLOAKER TO THE HOLE.
I'LL BE WATCHING YOU SPAWNS OF BITCHES, DON'T YOU WORRY.
MOVE IT.

...
THANKS, MON.

KUMICHO...

WE COME TO YOU WITH A DILEMMA. WE ARE IN CRISIS.

WE ARE FRACTURED AFTER THE BLOW WE SUFFERED LAST WEEK.

THE GREATEST KAIJU OF ALL, APE-WHALE, MURDERED BY AN UNKNOWN ASSASSIN.

NOW OUR MEMBERS ARE BEING ATTACKED WITH NO FEAR OF REPRISAL.

WE MAY EVEN LOSE THE KITCHEN WORK DETAIL.

THIS THING-FROM-OUTER-SPACE OF OURS NO LONGER INSPIRES TERROR AND RESPECT AMONG THE GENERAL POPULATION.

WE NEED STRENGTH KUMICHO. LEADERSHIP.

WE NEED HOPE.

WE NEED YOUR WISDOM.

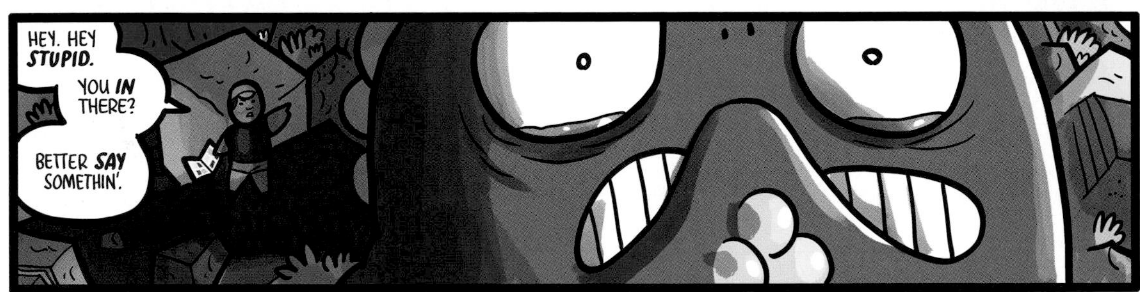
HEY. HEY **STUPID.**
YOU **IN** THERE?
BETTER **SAY** SOMETHIN'.

I-I-I--
I-I **THIRSTY.** C-CAN I HAVE A **DRINK?**
WELL, OF **COURSE,** BOSS, BUT...

IDIOT.
FOR GOJ'S **SAKE.** CAN'T YOU DO **ANY-THING?**
THEY'RE COMING TO YOU FOR **ANSWERS.** THEY'RE GIVING YOU ALL THIS **POWER.**
YOU NEED TO **DO** SOMETHING WITH IT.

BUT FIRST, YOU NEED TO COVER YOUR **TRACKS.** ARE YOU **LISTENING** TO ME?
THIS IS WHAT YOU'RE GOING TO **SAY**...

M-MY ESTEENED COLLEAGUES...
THE M-MURDER OF MY FATHER HANGS OVER US LIKE A R-R-RADIARATION CLOUD. IT MUST NOT GO UMPUNISHED.
WE WILL P-PAY BLOOD FOR BLOOD.
A-ALL ARE SUSPECT.
S-SEARCH IN OUR GROUP FOR ANY SIGN OF RIVALRY WITH MY FATHER, N-NO MATTER HOW LONG AGO, O-OR I-I-IMSIGNIFICAT IT SEEM.
THAT IS WH-WHERE OUR MURDERER IS HIDING.

B-BUT KUMICHO...
A-ALL OF US HAVE BATTLED YOUR FATHER AT ONE TIME OR ANOTHER.
THAT IS HOW WE MET HIM. AND HOW WE PROVED OUR WORTH AS EQUALS.
SURELY YOU DON'T WANT TO DIVIDE US JUST WHEN WE SHOULD BE WORKING TOGETH--
YES.
THAT IS THE ONLY W-WAY WE WILL FIND THE KILLER.

U-UNLESS YOU FEEL LIKE THIS SEARCH WILL DISCOVER SOMETHING UMPLEASANT ABOUT YOU, MONSTER X-ZERO.
N-NO!
O-OF COURSE NOT.
W-WE WILL DO AS YOU SAY, KUMICHO. YOUR WISDOM IS ABSOLUTE.

YES, THAT'S RIGHT.
SUCH A WISE, WISE LEADER.
LONG MAY HE REIGN.
"GUESS WHO?"

I KNOW WHO IT BETTER BE.
AND I KNOW WHAT SHE BETTER HAVE WITH HER.
HEY, BABE.

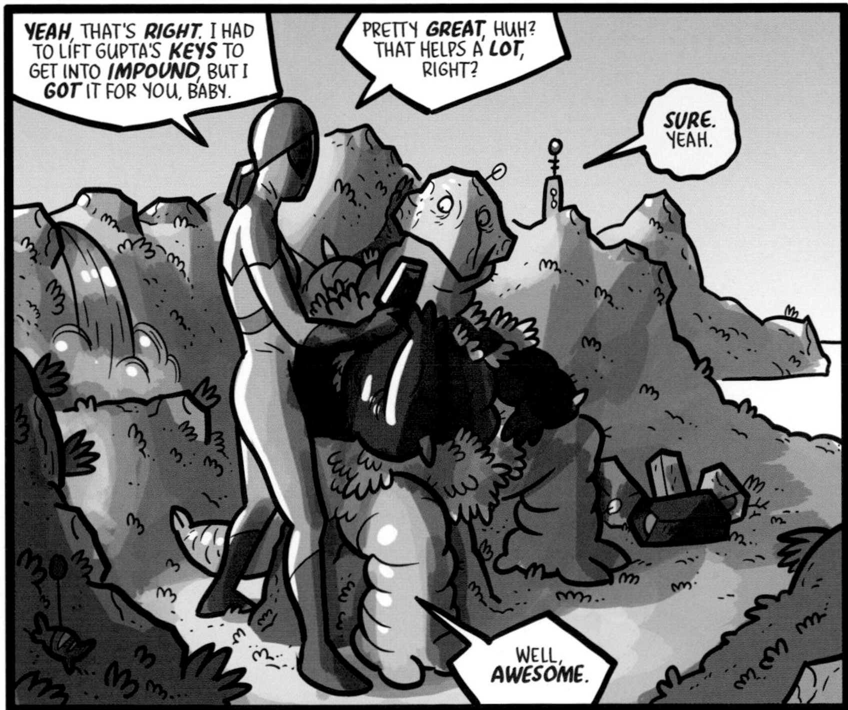

YEAH, THAT'S RIGHT. I HAD TO LIFT GUPTA'S KEYS TO GET INTO IMPOUND, BUT I GOT IT FOR YOU, BABY.
PRETTY GREAT, HUH? THAT HELPS A LOT, RIGHT?
SURE. YEAH.
WELL, AWESOME.

BOOP
BEEP
A-AND LOOK, IT STILL WORKS AND EVERY-THING.
I MADE SURE TO CHARGE IT.
a wild 3rd grader appears!
CAPTURE
EAT
Q
UH HUH.

IT'S JUST WHAT YOU WANTED, RIGHT? I DIDN'T FORGET ANY-THING?
NAH, IT'S GOOD.
BEEP
CAPTURED

HEY, YOU KNOW, YOU COULD SAY THANKS OR SOMETHING. I HAD TO WAIT TWO HOURS UNTIL SOME-ONE WASN'T WATCHING THOSE KEYS.
PFF!
I SAID IT WAS GOOD. WHAT DO YOU WANT, A 21-TANK SALUTE?
YOU DID WHAT YOU WERE SUPPOSED TO. WHOOP DEE DOO. NICE WORK, ZOOKY.

HEY!! WHAT THE--
ARE YOU KIDDING ME? BABY, I'M YOUR GIRL. I'M THE ONLY ONE LOOKING OUT FOR YOU. WATCHING YOUR BACK. GETTING YOU STUFF.
DO YOU KNOW WHAT WOULD HAPPEN IF I WERE CAUGHT FOR ANY ONE OF THOSE THINGS?
NAH.
YOU MADE YOUR OWN DECISIONS.
EXPLAIN THAT TO YOUR BOSS.
NOW MICTURATE OFF TO YOUR LITTLE JOB.
I GOT SOMEONE TO MEET.

MEET? WHO IS--
DON'T YOU DARE WALK AWAY FROM ME! DON'T YOU DARE!
HEY!

HEY!
ZONN! DO YOU HEAR ME?? YOU SPAWN OF A BITCH, COME BACK HERE AND TALK TO ME!
DO YOU HEAR ME?! I'M TALKING TO YOU!!
I SAID, DO YOU--

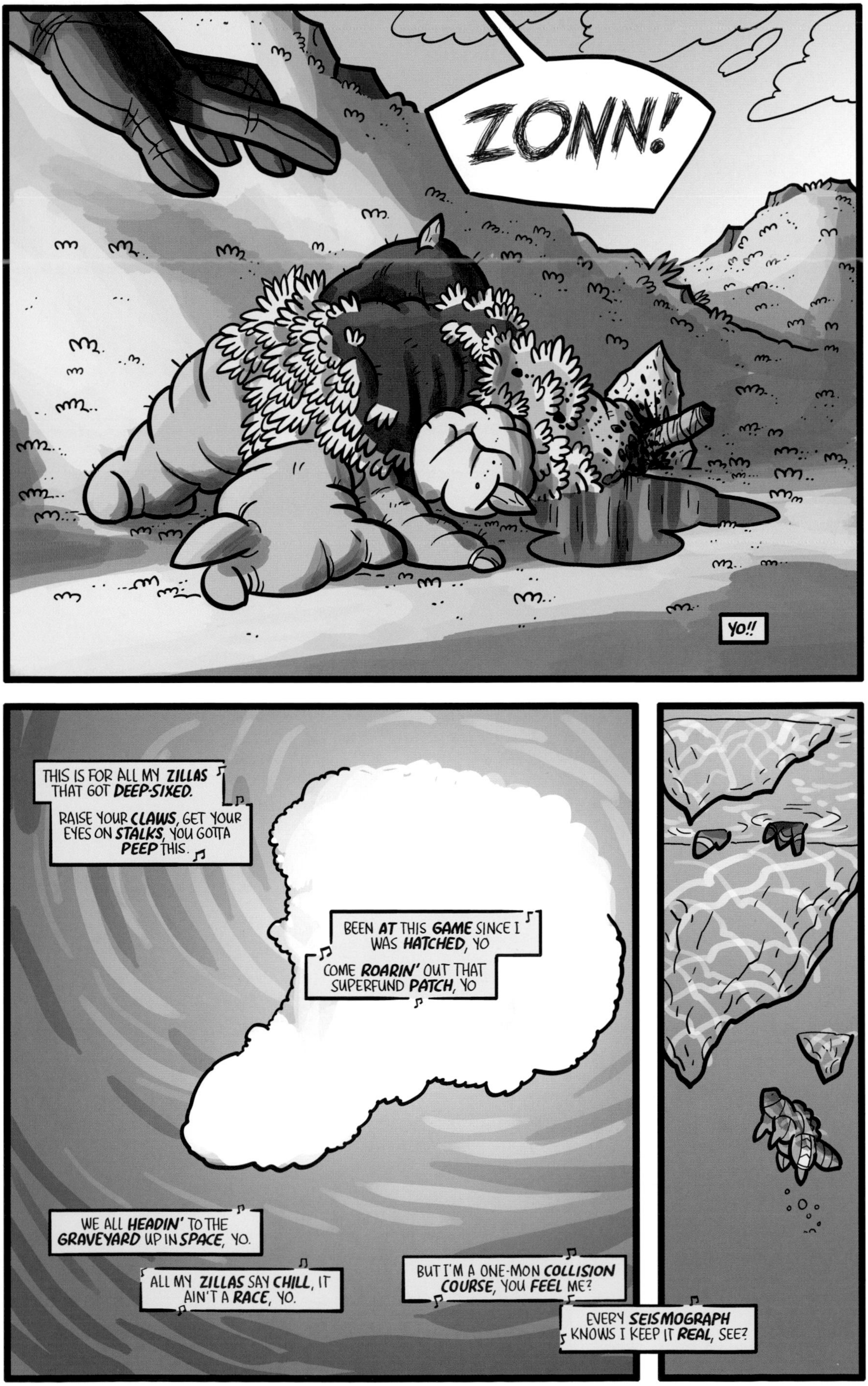

ZONN!

YO!!

THIS IS FOR ALL MY **ZILLAS** THAT GOT **DEEP-SIXED.**

RAISE YOUR **CLAWS**, GET YOUR EYES ON **STALKS**, YOU GOTTA **PEEP** THIS.

BEEN **AT** THIS **GAME** SINCE I WAS **HATCHED**, YO

COME **ROARIN'** OUT THAT SUPERFUND **PATCH**, YO

WE ALL **HEADIN'** TO THE **GRAVEYARD** UP IN **SPACE**, YO.

ALL MY **ZILLAS** SAY **CHILL**, IT AIN'T A **RACE**, YO.

BUT I'M A ONE-MON **COLLISION COURSE**, YOU **FEEL** ME?

EVERY **SEISMOGRAPH** KNOWS I KEEP IT **REAL**, SEE?

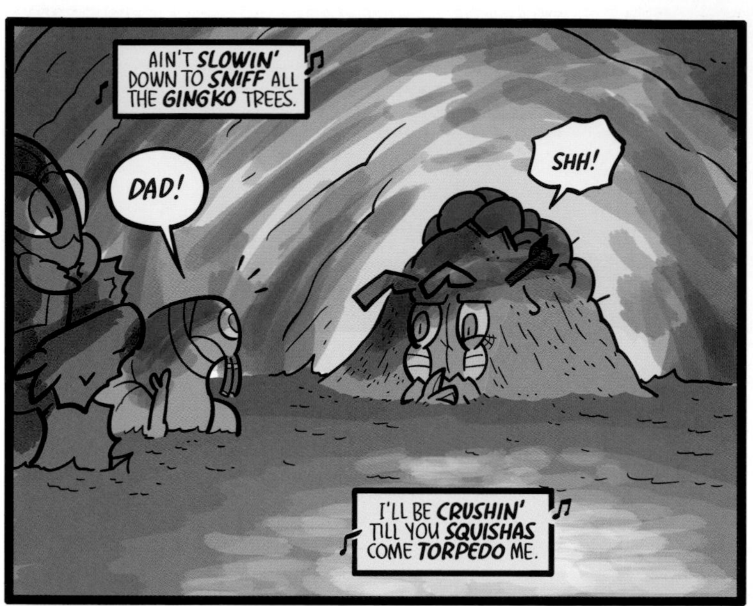
AIN'T SLOWIN' DOWN TO SNIFF ALL THE GINGKO TREES.
DAD!
SHH!
I'LL BE CRUSHIN' TILL YOU SQUISHAS COME TORPEDO ME.

NEVER GONNA STOP MOTION LIKE AN OCTOPUS--

I'M LOW-BUDGET LIVE-ACTION, YO, I'M ROCKIN' THIS.

WHEN IT'S MY TIME AND I MAKE IT TO THE THIRD REEL--
SHI-BOOYAH, MEGAFAUNA, THAT'S SOME COLD STEEL--
KNOCKED DOWN BROKEN, CRUSHED, AND EATIN' LEAD, YO
ELECTROCUTED, MASERED, NUKED UNTIL I'M DEAD, YO

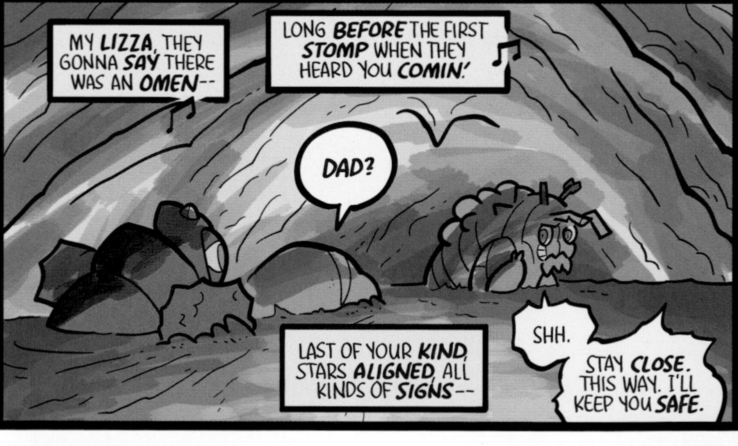
MY LIZZA, THEY GONNA SAY THERE WAS AN OMEN--
LONG BEFORE THE FIRST STOMP WHEN THEY HEARD YOU COMIN'
DAD?
LAST OF YOUR KIND, STARS ALIGNED, ALL KINDS OF SIGNS--
SHH.
STAY CLOSE. THIS WAY. I'LL KEEP YOU SAFE.

NO MATTER WHAT?
BUT WHAT THEY GONNA SAY 'BOUT THEM CRATERS YOU LEFT BEHIND?

NO MATTER **WHAT**.

HUH

HNNF
SCRTCH
SKTCH
YO, MON...

YOU LOOK LIKE YOU'RE **FEELIN'** BETTER.
GOT THAT **SPRING** BACK IN YOUR STOMP.
YEAH...
SCRATCH
SKTCH
WHAT'S GOIN' **ON**, YO? WHERE'S EVERYBODY **RUNNIN'** TO?
Y'KNOW **WHAT?**

I DON'T **CARE**.
THAT **PLAN** OF YOURS...
YOU NEED A BIG **ENERGY SOURCE**, RIGHT?
SKTCH
YEAH...?

WELL, YOU THINK 6 TONS OF **URANIUM** WILL DO IT?

"THAT'LL **WORK.**"

CAMERA 6
EJECT

ZZT

NO INPUT

SHING

ZOM

BLIP

WHO--

HHF OH GOD--
WAIT!
SHRIPP
WAIT!! I HAVE MONEY!!

PLEASE!! I HAVE MONEY!!

ENOUGH TO BUY A NEW PRINCE?
SHRIPP
MM!

MM!!

MM!

VIP
"I THINK HE'S GONE."

NO. KEEP DOING THOSE COMPRESSIONS.
DOCTOR, I DON'T THINK WE CAN SAVE HIM.
NO! WE ARE GOING TO SAVE HIM. YOU KEEP DOING THOSE COMPRESSIONS!

DR. ZHANG, THE WOUND IS TOO DEEP. HE'S LOSING TOO MUCH BLOOD.
NO. NO!
SHING
NO!

NO!
ZOOF

No, I am NOT going to LOSE you. I'm NOT.

HNFF Gotta FIND the ARTERY--

GUSH
GOT it-- HERE, now just--

HNFF--TIE it OFF--I GOT you, baby--
I GOT you--

Okay.
It's **OKAY** now.
I **GOT** you. We're **OKAY** now. **YOU** and **ME**.
I **LOVE** you.
I love you **SO MUCH**.
"THAT'S KIND OF... MESSED **UP**."

I MEAN, DETONATING AN **EXPLOSIVE** ON THE ISLAND? AREN'T ZILLAS GONNA GET **HURT?**
NAH, THIS BOMB'S MADE OF YOUR **JUNK** URANIUM, RIGHT? NO **OFFENSE**.
IT JUST HAS TO ZAP THE **PYLONS**. **INTERRUPT** 'EM FOR A SEC, NOT **EXPLODE** EVEN.
BLOCK

IF YOU **SAY** SO, MON ALL THAT **TECHNICAL** TALK IS BALTANESE TO **ME**.
HNNF
SCRATCH
SCRATCH
HEY, KEEP YOUR **ANTENNAE** UP.
WE GET **FIRE** ON THE LINE, I NEED TIME TO **HIDE** THIS.

WHAT ABOUT **CAMERAS?** ARE WE OUT OF **VIEW** ENOUGH FOR **THAT?**
SCRITCH
AAH, **SURVEILLANCE** IN THIS JOINT IS A TOTAL **AMBERGRIS-SHOW**.
FOR **REAL**, I GOT NO IDEA WHAT THEY'RE **DOING** IN THERE, BUT IT DON'T SEEM TO INVOLVE US **LIZZAS**

SO **CHILL**. I'M ALMOST **DONE**. AND STOP THAT **SCRATCHIN'**, YO, IT'S MAKIN' ME **NERVOUS**.
I CAN'T **HELP** IT. IT'S DRIVIN' ME **CRAZY**.

I THOUGHT YOU WAS FEELIN' **BETTER**.
I **AM**, KINDA. IT JUST--
IT **ITCHES** SO **BAD** NOW. IT'S LIKE...
NNG

NNG!
WHAT--
SKT
SKRTCH
GGHH

WHAT **IS** IT? **WHAT** ARE YOU--
SKTCH
SKUTCH

KRCH

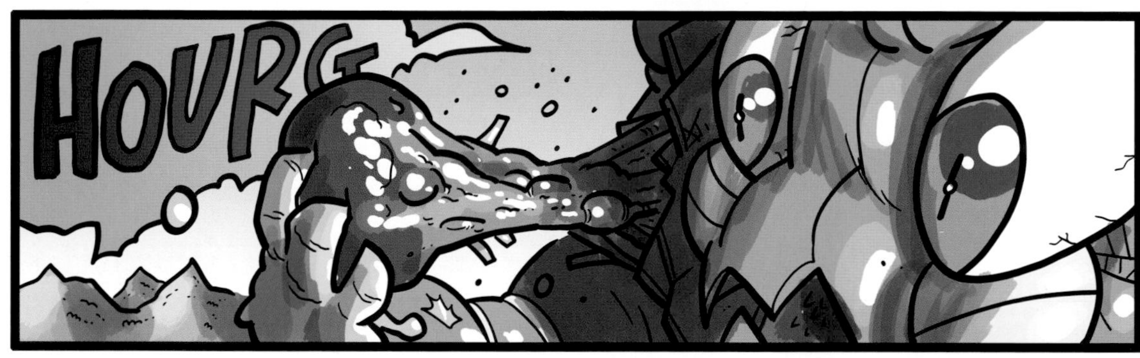
HOURG

HHUGH
OH MY--
SPLUT

HO-LY **DARVAZZA**, YO, WHAT IS **THAT?**
WHOA, YOU **SEE** THAT? IT ALMOST LOOKS LIKE THAT **NEW**--

...GUY...
!
STOMP

LET'S GET OUT OF THIS REDKING HOLE

...what I'm HEARING is that he's STABILIZED. We, uh, we're having TROUBLE rounding up all the SUSPECTS.

Whatever's made him a good STATE'S WITNESS has also made him a lot of ENEMIES here.
So with THAT, and the employee TURNOVER, well...
...things are in TRANSITION, Ma'am, but we're making PROGRESS.

Kang, I'm PLEASED that you are handling the UPS and DOWNS so well out there.
That I don't need to come DOWN and stick my NOSE in.

Well, THANK you, Dr. Matsu-moto.

That's really good to HEA--

Dr. **MATSUMOTO**, I have to call you **BACK**.

SHING

OH MY GOD.

THIS IS THE WARDEN.
WE HAVE AN UNAP-PROVED EXPLOSION AT DON BLOCK. POSSIBLE FORCEFIELD BREACH.
KEIKO, COME IN.
COME IN, ANYONE.

DAMN IT.

WARDEN, WHAT IS--
SECURE THE NORTH PERIMETER! ROUTE ALL PYLONS TO THE BACKUP GENERA-TORS!
PUT EVERY PRISONER IN LOCKDOWN. NO EXCEP-TIONS.

SNIFF

HOLY--
THEY DID IT!
YEAH, BUDDY!!
GO MON GO!!

NO

FORCEFIELDSZZXX
OFFLINEXXZZT

OKAY, SORRY ABOUT THAT.
LET'S GO.
END of SEASON ONE

怪獣
マックス
SOLITARY
CONFINEMENT
TSU
BLOCK
the
MALE PRISON at
KAIJUMAX
ISLAND
KANG JAE-YOON, WARDEN
"here be dragons"
COMMON
AREA
ha
ha
KITCHEN
OMG
WAH
EXERCISE YARD
INFIRMARY
WA
BLOCK
ウ6ス
17.371966 S
177.136123 E
ART BY
Kevin Cannon
BASED ON CARTOGRAPHICAL
NOTES STOLEN FROM THE
STUDIO OF ZANDER CANNON
N
S

Kaiju Max
KAI BLOCK
VISITORS
HEADQUARTERS
IN TAKE
KI BLOCK
SHOWERS
ENTRANCE
DON BLOCK

COMING SOON
in
KAIJUMAX
SEASON TWO

THE VIOLENCE AND MISERY CONTINUES ON A GLOBAL SCALE!

ELECTROGOR ENCOUNTERS SERIOUS OBSTACLES TO FINDING HIS CHILDREN, AND THE **GREEN HUMONGO** GETS A NASTY SURPRISE ABOUT WHAT HAPPENED TO HIS ELECTRICITY-DEALING PATCH BACK HOME.

KAIJUMAX GOES INTO LOCKDOWN AS REPAIR BEGINS, OVERSEEN BY **WARDEN KANG** AND THE NO-NONSENSE **H.E.R.O.I.S.M.** ADMINISTRATOR **DR. MATSUMOTO.**

AND

ENTHUSIASTIC ROOKIE COP **CHISATO** GETS HER FIRST ASSIGNMENT: TRACK DOWN, APPREHEND, AND RETURN THE FUGITIVE PRISONERS.

WANTED

AFTER ROAR

This book represents a lot of decisions I resisted making for many years.

I resisted working for smaller press publishers. I resisted creating ambitious new series. I resisted writing and drawing a series by myself. I certainly resisted coloring it, and most of all, I resisted doing anything on a monthly schedule.

I resisted all those things because they were inefficient, because they didn't pay well, or because other people didn't think they were the smart thing to do. Perhaps they aren't. Perhaps it does make a lot more sense to write several series than write and draw one. Or to do little freelance illustration gigs while spending years on a graphic novel. I know I've joked with many people that writing, drawing, lettering, and coloring* an ostensibly monthly comic book is a questionable move. But nothing I've ever done has made me happier.

To hear people tell it, monster movies are silly. Prison movies are lurid. And for that matter, comic books are dumb. But I love all of them to varying degrees, and I have reached a place in my career that I can choose to ignore the prevailing aesthetic opinions, and instead just do something that makes me happy. I spent many years doing work that I thought was "important", and I believe some of it was, but for all its importance it never made me half as happy as I am when I'm drawing monsters taking drugs and murdering each other.

I compulsively read reviews and reactions to this comic. I don't for everything. If I've just written or just drawn a book, I have very little interest in what people think about my contribution, because a) it's rare that one can tell where one collaborator leaves off and the other begins, and b) not many people comment in a way about writing or artistic technique that is meaningful or helpful to me as a creator. But everyone that reads a book has reactions. And on Kaijumax, as the instigator of those reactions, I am always hungry to know what they are. A review that communicates joy, pity, hatred, disgust, laughter (or my favorite, all of the above), whether good or bad, is like a filling meal to me.

To have created something that people react to is the primary goal of the artist. I resisted it for many years out of the fear of failure, the fear of irrelevance, the fear of not making enough money, and the fear of looking foolish. If you have been resisting something for the same reasons, my advice to you is: try it.

It might be the best decision you've ever made.

---

*with help from Jason Fischer, of course.

SINCE 1993, ***ZANDER CANNON*** HAS WRITTEN AND DRAWN COMICS ABOUT GODS, ROBOTS, ASTRONAUTS, POLICE OFFICERS, PALEONTOLOGISTS, ALIENS, FENG SHUI MASTERS, SUPERHEROES, AND MONSTERS.

HE LIVES IN MINNESOTA WITH HIS STRONG WIFE JULIE AND ABOVE-AVERAGE SON JIN.

KAIJUMAX.COM
@ZANDER_CANNON

WHERE YOU BEEN? DID YOUR ICEBERG JUST CRACK? 'CUZ I'M HERE TO THROW DOWN ANOTHER MEGA-MONSTER DISS TRACK.
WHEN I COME STOMPIN' OUT THE BIG HOUSE, PEOPLE GONNA SCATTER. "YO, THAT LIZZA'S SPITTIN' FLAME LIKE IT DON'T MATTER!" THINK IT'S THE FIRST TIME I SEEN A MASER ON AN ARMY TRUCK? FOOL, I BEEN AROUND THE WORLD MORE TIMES THAN THEM RUBBER DUCKS.
SO I'M CALLIN' OUT THE BIG MON. YOU HEARD ME UP THERE, WAVIN' YOUR ARMS AT THE PLANES LIKE YOU DON'T CARE. YOU THINK YOU'RE THE BEAST, BUT I'LL BE THE ONE TO TELL YA: YOUR GAME IS SO WEAK THAT I SAW BEAUTY COME AND KILL YA.
AND THE O.G. OVER HERE, TOP A' THE HEAP UNTIL '05. NOW Y'LOOKIN' TOO FAT FOR OTAKU ON THE EAST SIDE. THINK YOU COME BACK HARD AFTER A DECADE OF COASTIN'? WHY DON'T YOU DO A CANNONBALL TO THE BOTTOM OF THE OCEAN?
JUST ABOUT TO BLEVE, AIN'T GONNA BE NO DOUBT. AIN'T ENOUGH YELLOW JUICE IN THE WORLD TO KEEP ME OUT. JUST IN CASE YOU DAMN SQUISHERS GONE AND MISSED IT...
YO, THIS TRACK IS FIRE, LIKE YOUR CITY'S WHARF DISTRICT.